Wisdom in Exile

Other books by Lama Jampa Thaye

A Garland of Gold
Essentials of Tibetan Buddhism
Diamond Sky
River of Memory
Rain of Clarity

Wisdom in Exile

Buddhism and Modern Times

Lama Jampa Thaye

Published by Dechen Foundation, 2017

Dechen Foundation is an association of Sakya and Karma Kagyu Buddhist centers founded by Lama Jampa Thaye under the authority of Karma Thinley Rinpoche. For more information, visit us at dechen.us

Library of Congress Control Number: 2017936287

Paperback ISBN: 978-0-9987507-2-9

eBook ISBN: 978-0-9987507-3-6

Cover design by Ian Savage

Author photograph by Andrew Gourley

Dedicated to my lamas

Contents

Foreword by HH the 41ˢᵗ Sakya Trizin   ix

Foreword by HH the 17ᵗʰ Karmapa   xi

Foreword by Karma Thinley Rinpoche   xiii

Introduction   xv

Chapter 1: Meetings   1

Chapter 2: The Space for Buddhism   7

Chapter 3: Science   21

Chapter 4: Politics   29

Chapter 5: Conceit   45

Chapter 6: Disillusionment   53

Chapter 7: Learning the Craft   65

Chapter 8: Meditation   73

Chapter 9: Wise Compassion   81

Chapter 10: Beginnings   107

Glossary of terms   109

List of names   113

Notes   117

Foreword
by
HH the 41ˢᵗ Sakya Trizin

His Holiness
Sakya Trizin
HEAD OF THE SAKYAPA ORDER
OF TIBETAN BUDDHISM

Dolma Phodrang
192 Rajpur Road,
P.O. Rajpur 248009
Dehra Dun U.A. INDIA

I am very pleased that this inspiring new book by Lama Jampa Thaye is being published.

Wisdom in Exile proposes a fresh approach to Buddhism, one in which the fundamental tenets of the Buddha's teachings are rediscovered. With the popularity that Buddhism has gained in the West over the past decades, it is essential to ensure that it remains true to its source.

In his book, Lama Jampa Thaye suggests that we re-examine our motivation in following Buddhism, making sure that our deepest aim is to attain liberation for the sake of all beings, and that our core practice is the cultivation of ethics, wisdom and compassion.

Wisdom in Exile provides excellent advice on how to avoid wrong views regarding Buddhism and how to build infallible foundations for our practice.

I pray that this work may bring precious guidance to students of the dharma and help them to swiftly progress on their path to liberation.

The Sakya Trizin
Sakya Dolma Phodrang, Rajpur, India
20th January 2017

Foreword
by
HH the 17ᵗʰ Karmapa
Trinley Thaye Dorje

The 17ᵗʰ Karmapa Trinley Thaye Dorje

Dear readers,

It is my pleasure to contribute a short foreword to Lama Jampa Thaye's latest publication, *Wisdom in Exile*.

Lama Jampa Thaye is a meditation master and scholar of both the Sakya and Kagyu traditions of Tibetan Buddhism, and as such has undergone rigorous traditional training with his Tibetan teachers.

At the same time, he is a Westerner and has been brought up in a Western environment. As such, he understands the mentality and background of Western students of the Buddha dharma.

Over the past few decades, Buddhism – and particularly Tibetan Buddhism – has attracted a great many followers in the West. While the students are genuine in their devotion and dedication to their freshly discovered spiritual path, most of them are relatively new to the teachings of Buddhism. This may lead them to misguidedly believe that the tenets of their own cultural and spiritual traditions and the actual teachings of Buddhism are one and the same.

Therefore, I think that this book will be beneficial in helping Western practitioners to avoid some of the pitfalls of cultural and spiritual misunderstanding.

May it be of benefit to countless beings!

With prayers

The 17th Karmapa Trinley Thaye Dorje
New Delhi
15th February 2017

Foreword
by
Karma Thinley Rinpoche

༄། མཁས་དབང་བླ་མ་བྱམས་པ་ མཐའ་ཡས་ཀྱིས་གསར་རྩོམ་མཛད་པའི་ལེགས་བཤད་འདི་ཡིས་ཤར་ནུབ་ཏུ་འཕེར་བའི་ནང་པའི་རྗེས་འཇུག་རྣམས་ལ་བླང་དོར་གྱི་ལམ་སྟོན་ཡོང་ངེས་ལགས་པས། དེ་བཞིན་དོན་དང་དོན་མིན་དབྱེ་འབྱེད་གལ་ཆེ་བ་བྱུ། ཅེས་པའང་། ཤཱཀྱའི་རྗེས་འཇུག་ཀརྨ་ཕྲིན་ལས་བཞི་པའམ། དཔལ་ལྡན་ས་སྐྱ་པ་ཆེན་པོས་སྐུ་ལ་མིང་དབང་བསྡུད་ནོར་བུའི་སྙིང་པོ་ཞེས་བགྱི་བས་བྲིས་པ་དགེ།

The scholar Lama Jampa Thaye has recently composed this text so that those following the Buddhist teaching newly established in the West may be certain concerning the paths to be adopted and rejected. Since it is very important to discriminate between the authentic and inauthentic, please pay attention to it.

Written by the follower of the Buddha who is known as the Fourth Karma Thinley, or, according to the Great Sakyapa, known as Wangdu Norbu Nyingpo.

Introduction

We live in a time when it can appear that the road to wisdom has been lost and its very existence forgotten. In its place is merely a dead-end street full of stale ideologies. Yet the path that Buddha set forth some two-and-a-half millennia ago is still there for us, even in these modern times, if we care to find it.

This present work is essentially a series of essays on the encounter between Buddhist teachings and the West. However, it is not a formal introduction to Buddhism nor a systematic exposition of Buddhist thought. There are many of these available. Neither does it claim to represent the whole of Buddhism. Inevitably, it reflects my understanding of the particular set of teachings and practices in which I have been trained by my Tibetan masters.

Buddhism itself developed out of the teachings given by the warm and friendly South Asian prince known to his followers as 'The Sage of the Shakyas'.[1] At the heart of these teachings is the insight that suffering arises primarily from our mistaken ideas about ourselves and the nature of the world – errors that prompt the arising of a confluence of disturbing emotions and actions. According to Buddha, liberation from suffering is always possible, through the transformation of our error into understanding, brought about by training in the three-fold path of ethics, meditation and wisdom. Thus, despite its ancient origins, Buddhism would seem to be uniquely well suited to the modern world.

The first half of this work considers the space that now exists for Buddhism in our culture. This is a space that has been opened up by the failure of our dominant systems of thought to provide an intelligent account of what it is to be human and how we should conduct ourselves in this world.

However, although this space exists, if Buddhism is to fill it effectively, the temptation to assimilate it to contemporary ideologies must be resisted. Nothing could be more destructive for Buddhism in the long run. With this point in mind, the latter chapters of this book consider how best the Buddha's teachings might be understood and practised today. There has been considerable enthusiasm directed to these subjects, but it is vital that we discriminate between authentic and fake presentations, the latter being those proffered by self-appointed authorities, which are thus unconnected with the unbroken traditions of teaching and practice, and, furthermore, whose presentations are refuted by direct experience or reasoning.

All too often, through a mixture of conceit and credulity, we have settled for the latter. Unfortunately, if we persist in getting Buddhism wrong in this way, the opportunity for it to shape our lives will be lost and Buddhism itself is likely to remain in cultural memory as nothing more than a temporary fad – another Theosophy.

Wisdom in Exile draws from the teachings I have received over the past five decades from His Holiness the 41st Sakya Trizin, Karma Thinley Rinpoche and various other Tibetan teachers, and, as such, it refers extensively to works composed by eminent masters of the Buddhist tradition. Therefore I've included a list of these masters at the end of this book, if only to make their names a little better known.

Some elements of this work have appeared in the online and print editions of Tricycle, while some other sections have featured in teachings given in Los Angeles and Dhagpo Kagyu Ling in France.

Thanks to Peter Popham and Liz Nash for their help in this project, and, as always, to my wife Albena and family. Thanks also to Ed Curtis, Adrian O'Sullivan and my editor Benjamin Lister.

Lama Jampa Thaye
Sakya Changlochen Ling, France
18th August 2016

Chapter 1
Meetings

It's 21st June 1974, and I'm standing in the doorway of the Buddhist Society in London, a big fine Georgian town house close to Victoria Station. On one side of me is a young Tibetan lama, Chime Rinpoche, and, on the other, is His Honour Judge Christmas Humphreys QC, the President of the Society, and an imposing figure as befits an Old Bailey judge. We are there to greet His Holiness the 41st Sakya Trizin, the twenty-eight-year-old head of the Sakya tradition of Tibetan Buddhism, on his first visit to England. The Buddhist Society and the Tibet Relief Fund have organised a reception in his honour, and Rinpoche has told me I can tag along.

After a few minutes, His Honour turns to Rinpoche, wanting to check the title of the person he is to welcome. At that same moment, a car pulls up and out steps His Holiness with an easy smile. He's accompanied by a couple of monks and two European ladies.

After we have shuffled upstairs to the reception room, Mr Humphreys delivers a speech of welcome, during which he highlights at length his part in the forming of the Society back in 1924 and his own unique role as the first person in history to discern the twelve essential principles of Buddhism. Discreet mention is also made of the President's deep friendship with His Holiness the Dalai Lama, to whom His Honour had been able to impart much sage advice. As the speech goes on, my mind drifts back to my very first visit to a Buddhist Society function some three years earlier. An English monk, the Venerable Pannavadho, had presided over the celebrations of Buddha's birthday, but, although Pannavadho himself was eminently serious and the Society's members were obviously sincere, it didn't seem like much of a celebration to me at the time. My companion's head was exploding and we had to make it out of there fast. The place, all mahogany and boredom, was so stuffy, I could hardly breathe.

My English Literature teacher, Mr Campbell, had set me on this road. It was 1966, and I was fourteen years old, a pupil at a Catholic Grammar school in the northern English city of Manchester: a grey place in a grey time. It was still the aftermath of the Second World War. British society was only just emerging from the hardness of those years, but something was active in the culture that would, among other things, help open a door for Buddhism. It was at the end of a class on *Julius Caesar* when this mighty colossus of a schoolmaster told me that someone who admired Bob Dylan as much as I did would certainly like Jack Kerouac: and so it turned out. I entered the world of the 'Beat Generation' writers through his books like *On the Road* and *Dharma Bums*, immediately realising that Dylan had been there already. Even more importantly, although Kerouac's work was tinged with a working-class Catholic sensibility with which I was very familiar, I discovered Buddhism there. I knew right away that I had found my way home.

While I was somewhat devout as a child, I already had a sense that the God of Catholicism was just too small. Whatever blessings and spiritual power had existed in the Church seemed to have evaporated long ago. Although in my early years I had felt repeated experiences of bliss and light, I couldn't connect them with anything I heard at church or in school. As time went by, I started to have powerful experiences where names, thoughts, and even time itself, seemed to be utterly empty. It was a world – the real world – from which one might return as an exile to the shadowy world of everyday life, but which would always be there. I could barely speak of these experiences, and any attempt to articulate them was useless, although I tried.

After a while, I gave up trying. I didn't expect anybody, whether my parents, teachers or priest, to understand, and they did not. Now, through Kerouac's words, I heard of the luminous emptiness that is the heart of all things. At last I had some context for my experiences, and I would be a Buddhist from that moment on. Yet six years would pass before I would start to practise it seriously.

Instead, imagining that I might find Buddhism, I came in at the tail end of the Beat Generation. It was really long over, even in Greenwich Village, its original location, and San Francisco, the places you might find some fading echoes of the Beats, but I tried to pick up their trail in the coffee houses of Manchester. There were a few poets around, and a guy who was rumoured to sell peyote, but there wasn't much else. By the end of 1967, I had made it as far as London, visiting the Arts Lab in Covent Garden and Indica bookshop on Southampton Row, ground zero of the 'underground' scene, where I bought a copy of *The Tibetan Book of the Dead*. Right around the corner was a shop selling Japanese incense. In the back room there was somebody called Sangharakshita, who was busy founding his own school of Buddhism. I didn't go in that back room, though – karma, I guess.

Although I left home and school a year later, still chasing the visions of Kerouac, Ginsberg, Snyder and the other Beat writers, I never really found what I had imagined would be there. From time to time, I met people who were searching for the same things. A few of them are still around today, but, as the years slipped by, that world grew darker. Sooner or later, everything became drugs or politics, and, after a while, I discovered that I wasn't really all that interested in either of them. Thinking back over this period of the so-called 'Alternative Society', it seems to me now that the same message that some heard as meaning that one should become 'free from self', others heard as indicating that one should 'free the self'. One way leads to Buddha, and the other to Aleister Crowley or Mao Tse Tung. Perhaps it was easy to confuse them in those days.

Eventually, I had to admit that there was nothing truthful in those places: just the ravenous self-love that roars out today in the million locations that make up contemporary culture. Some of us may have started from the right spot, but we were now on a wide road that led only downwards. As for the Beats themselves, they were long gone. I would meet up with Allen Ginsberg, though, several years later. By then, he was a disciple of Trungpa Rinpoche, one of the first popularisers of Tibetan Buddhism in the United States.

It was in late 1972 that I came in from the wilderness and started to get serious about Buddhism. Initially I practised in the Theravada tradition, where I met the wise old-timer Russell Williams and the scholar Lance Cousins. However, within a couple of years, I had found the two Tibetan lamas who would be my masters for life: His Holiness the 41st Sakya Trizin (1945–) and Karma Thinley Rinpoche (1931–). Thanks to them, over the next several decades, I received some of the elements of a traditional Buddhist education, primarily the contemplative and philosophical teachings of the Sakya and Kagyu schools.

In the meantime, my academic life began in 1973, when, two months after meeting Karma Thinley Rinpoche, I embarked upon a degree in Religious Studies at the University of Manchester. I didn't realise it at the time, but it would eventually stretch to a BA, a PhD, and twenty years of teaching at the two universities in Manchester. I was trained there as a historian of religions by such eminent professors as Trevor Ling. However, I have to confess that academic work was just a way to support my Buddhist studies, practice and retreats. It's not, incidentally, that I think that such academic scholarship isn't worthy of respect, but I just didn't want to get too caught up in it. I had other things to do.

Chapter 2

The Space for Buddhism

The Buddhism that I discovered through the Beats was not entirely new in the West. In fact, it had been entering it for over a century without great fanfare, whether through Asian immigrant communities, Western scholarship or converts. Ironically enough, during the very period of the 20th and 21st centuries when Western culture and values have seemed triumphant, a spiritual decay at the heart of this culture appears to have created an opening for Buddhism. The story of how this has happened is of some importance.

It starts with loss. Our culture seems to be one that is haunted by it. It is as if we modern men and women have lost our sense of place in the world, our place in the very rhythms of birth and death. At this time when people measure their lives in terms of popularity and fame, it sometimes seems that nothing of value remains. Fleeting passions and manias infest people's minds with images and distorted facts. It is as if we are living in a valley of dry bones where the only noises are the rustle of yesterday's newspaper with its story of an already-forgotten celebrity and the voice of Big Brother sounding from the electronic screen. Consequently, we are forever chasing happiness, hoping to find it in the forgetfulness of pleasure. Similarly, not knowing who we are, we seek confirmation of our identity through the chatter of social media. However, we find in either place only frustration and insecurity.

Of course, as Buddha pointed out, suffering afflicts all sentient beings and hence is undoubtedly present in all cultures. However, maybe our culture is unique in selling the promise of happiness so strongly but delivering only disappointment and bewilderment.

To understand how this has come to pass, we have to begin with the past. In other words, we must ask, in the fashion of Buddhist reasoning: 'What are the causes and conditions which have given rise to the apparent phenomenon of our deracinated and dissatisfied culture?'

To begin, one might concede that the Renaissance was undoubtedly significant in shaping some of our contemporary sensibilities. This recovery of the best elements of Classical civilisation produced, in the fourteenth to sixteenth centuries, a culture that was focussed on man 'as the measure of all things' – part of a shift towards modern individualism. However, it is probably more accurate to say that modern Western culture began with the sixteenth-century Reformation. It was this cataclysm that shattered the world of mediaeval Catholic Christianity in Western Europe, a culture which, despite its many faults, had nurtured a sense of the unity of the sacred and secular, and thus given men and women a secure notion of their rootedness in the world.

At the heart of the mediaeval vision was a notion of a cosmic order into which humankind was folded. It was a hierarchy comprising humans, saints, angelic orders and God, and, of course, the denizens of purgatory and hell. Reflecting the vastness of this vision, the Catholic culture of the time was spacious enough to accommodate everything from the scholarship of the monastic orders to the devotional cults of the peasantry, from Dante's *Divine Comedy* to Chaucer's *Canterbury Tales*.

In 1517, the German Protestant Reformer, Martin Luther (1483–1546) – followed, a few years later, by Jean Calvin (1509–1564) in Geneva – shattered the world of

Catholic Christianity. Luther and Calvin's new theology eliminated devotion to the saints, jettisoned purgatory, abolished the monastic orders and dispensed with the role of the priesthood as the intermediary between man and God. Through removing these structures that securely located the individual life within a spiritual and social context which was greater than the mere individual, the two Reformers broke the chain that had connected the sacred and the temporal. It seems also that, in insisting on the absolute privacy of the individual conscience alone before God, they unintentionally gave rise to a new alienated individualism, for, from now on, humanity would be cut off from the mediating assistance of the priest and saints.[2]

To this interior transformation of what it was to be religious, Calvin added the sanctification of work, through his notion that one's profession was a divine calling or 'vocation', and this, together with his depiction of wealth as a sign of divine favour bestowed only upon those who had been chosen by God, brought into being a culture that was remarkably favourable to the growth of a capitalist economy. In due course, these cultural and economic shifts would sweep away the mediaeval ordering of society, together with its religious forms.[3]

In this way, the old spiritual world was fractured, and our sense of having a place within an ordered cosmos was lost. From that time onward, Christianity, even in its new guise – and despite the ambitions of the Protestant Reformers – has only continued to cede territory and authority to other blueprints for meaning and happiness, most notably those stemming from the worlds of politics and science. However, strangely enough, in these two systems, one may still discern the ghost of Christianity, as we shall see.

In recent times, political ideology has thus come to enjoy some of the unquestioning faith that was previously accorded to religion. The roots of such a development actually lie in the Reformation itself, when Luther's attack on the hierarchical authority of Catholic Christianity in matters of religion soon spilled over into a demand by Anabaptists and other revolutionary Millenarians that society and authority should be levelled: a re-ordering that they associated with the return of Christ and his thousand-year kingdom over which he would rule together with the just. Although the German Peasants' Revolt of 1525 and the various uprisings of the subsequent decade in Europe were crushed, they were harbingers of what was to come.[4]

In the event, it would take nearly three centuries for a revolutionary movement finally to succeed in its aim of a total reconstitution of society, when the French Revolutionaries seized power at the end of the eighteenth century. However, by this time, the essentially apocalyptic Christian view of history that had been revolution's initial impulse had been obscured. Revolution was to be, from then on, in the hands of the officially secular and anti-religious. Nevertheless, all revolutionary movements up to the present day are, in important respects, still indebted to Millenarian Christian views. All these movements anticipate an apocalypse that will consume the unrighteous and be followed by the age of perfection to be enjoyed by the just – as, indeed, the post-Reformation movements had envisioned.

Despite the aspirations of its devotees, who are still highly influential in our culture, utopia has not put in an appearance. Its failure to do so should alert us to the intrinsic and inescapable flaw in this pattern of thought: its externalisation of the search for perfection. Contrary to what political ideologies assert, a totally positive re-ordering of society cannot take place in the absence of an interior transformation. Unless the actual roots of the suffering that we inflict upon ourselves and others are dissolved in the individual heart, political action is, at best, doomed to disappoint, and is more often likely to be disastrous. In short, as Buddha taught, it is only by cultivating a freedom from the tyranny of selfishness through sustained attention to ethics, meditation and wisdom that any engagement with the world can be well-founded. This is a point to which we will return in Chapter 4.

By contrast, political ideologies, even those which seem benevolent in their intentions, rely for their energy upon the notion of external enemies – often, one suspects, to spare their followers the challenge of the confrontation with the enemy within. We see this time after time, when at last the revolution, having warred first with its visible enemies, finally consumes its own children, as in the French Revolutionary Terror of the 1790s. Again, we will have cause to say more about this later.

If, in recent centuries, political ideologies have offered many a supposed route to happiness, science provides another. The rise of science itself is usually associated with the intellectual climate of the seventeenth and eighteenth centuries, the 'Age of Reason' and the 'Age of Enlightenment' respectively. In those centuries, a new type of thinker achieved prominence: the 'intellectual' or 'free thinker', who came to replace the Church-sanctioned scholar, priest or minister as the new figure of prestige and authority.[5] Yet this development too, as with the rise of a political culture, also has roots in the Reformation. There, Luther's insistence on the primacy of the individual conscience, informed only by the Bible and not by tradition, was a first step towards the creation of a free-thinking intellectual, even though Luther had intended only a new orthodoxy.

Even the free thinkers of the seventeenth century did not start off as explicitly anti-religious. The greatest of them, René Descartes (1596–1650), hoped, as a loyal Catholic, to endow theism with a sure defence when he argued that the existence and nature of God could be determined solely by the free exercise of reason.[6] In so doing, he contradicted St

Thomas Aquinas,[7] perhaps the greatest of Christian thinkers, who, despite his Aristotelianism, had ruled that some matters were still the domain only of revelation and inaccessible to reason.

Unfortunately for Descartes, just as Luther before him, his work would have entirely unintended consequences. Luther had failed to anticipate that, in making the Bible available to all, he would merely ensure that now there would be hundreds of different interpretations of Scripture, culminating in one that would reject it entirely. So too, Descartes did not foresee the consequences of his innovation. He had failed to anticipate that, by the end of the eighteenth century, the free exercise of reason would reach its inevitable apotheosis in the work of truly post-Christian thinkers such as Voltaire, Rousseau and Hume, who would respectively use it to satirise religious authority, plan for an entirely secular society and demolish any case for God's manifestation in nature.

Thus, by the nineteenth century, Christianity, whether Catholic or Protestant, was a defeated and discredited force among the opinion makers of the West. The notion was by now firmly entrenched that, through the application of reason to the natural world in scientific analysis, nature could be forced to yield up its secrets. Any sense of a sacred presence in nature – one demonstrated in mediaeval Catholicism by its shrines and other holy places – had been banished, first by the iconoclasm of the Protestant Reformation and now by the new science. Thus grew the belief that the physical world, society and, finally, the mind itself, could all be understood and re-ordered on rational lines, and, with this, suffering would be banished. In short, the idea of the scientist as a kind of substitute God – who has assumed powers previously ascribed by Christianity to the Creator – was now in place, as slyly dissected in Mary Shelley's *Frankenstein* early in the nineteenth century.[8]

There were, of course, dissenters from this mood of optimism, but even they, whether Romantics, or, some time later, Nietzsche, felt that modern humankind lived in an irredeemably de-sacralised world and was, likewise, forever cut off from the continuity of human experience present in tradition. Relatively few, such as the English poet William Blake (1757–1827), seem not to have completely accepted this.

In such a way, scientific praxis became illegitimately wedded to an ideology that might more properly be termed 'scientism'.[9] Although scientism claims the authority of science, it has as many unexamined assumptions as any form of theism. The roots of this grim alchemical wedding between science and ideology lie in the anti-religious philosophical materialism that grew steadily throughout the seventeenth, eighteenth and nineteenth centuries and now enjoys considerable popularity amongst those who regard themselves as both fashionable and intellectual.

In an amusing parallel to the optimism of the political ideologues concerning their utopian societies, devotees of this scientistic ideology confidently anticipate the day when the 'problem of consciousness' will be solved and all will be forced to accept the materialist thesis. In the meantime, any beneficial advances, such as, for instance, in medical care and treatment, properly due to the application of genuine scientific praxis by scientists, can be falsely claimed for materialism.

It is essential to be clear about this point: the analysis to determine which particular physical processes are implicated in a particular disorder or disease, and, likewise, the formulation of specific remedies, does not entail a commitment to any one particular world-view of the ultimate nature of reality. Hence, the medical researcher may be Christian, Jewish, materialist or Buddhist, as scientific praxis is merely based upon the observation and understanding of how particular causes and conditions interact to produce particular effects in a given situation.

However, it is by this illegitimate stratagem of disguising itself as science that scientism attempts to maintain its prestige. In this regard, it is noteworthy that it is particularly popular among those who are often untutored in science but may be hostile to religion for other reasons.

Just as surely as the blindness in political vision has had unfortunate consequences, so also with the scientistic ideology. Unchecked, there is every possibility that it will render sentient beings into mere scientific specimens, whose defects and malfunctions it imagines can be eliminated and whose lives are to be managed from the time of controlled conception to controlled death. Its ambitions are such that it is determined to deny that human beings have consciousness and moral agency, by asserting that they are mere physical matter which acts in accordance with environmental conditions. Of course, such an approach will leave intact the fundamental causes of suffering: causes which reside in the human heart itself.

When one adds to these flaws of scientism and political ideology the danger to the human capacity for stillness, reflection and wise judgement that is signalled by the proliferation of electronic media to satisfy our immediate desires, one can easily understand why it is that our culture can appear to be spiritually bankrupt. Although it has made some advances, in many ways it has only added to the sum total of unhappiness and alienation. So, what is to be done?

The first step is to admit that the solution to this crisis in modern culture is not to imagine that we can turn back the clock and all will be well. In other words, a voluntary return to theism (the belief in a creator god), in order to recover the lost unity of the sacred and secular, is not possible for most people. Freedom of thought has already exposed much that seems incoherent in theistic belief. In addition, a great deal of religious practice in the West has been fatally damaged. The very facts that popular devotion is increasingly moribund outside of certain redoubts, or that once-great monastic orders face continual shrinkage, only confirm that sombre analysis. Thus, with all due apologies to the great T.S. Eliot, who decided that salvation for the individual and the culture could only be found in the embrace of Christian tradition, there is little reason to look for aid there.

It is this fact, then, that creates a space in our culture for Buddhism, a system which, unlike its spiritual rivals, can create confidence by its very accessibility to reasoning – an accessibility made possible by its sophisticated traditions of logical enquiry and philosophical analysis. It was Buddha himself who set the tone for this in his well-known dictum that his teaching was not to be accepted through blind faith. Instead he insisted that, just as a merchant first tests the weight and purity of gold before purchasing it, so one should assess the veracity of his teachings for oneself before giving assent to them.

In the centuries after the Buddha, this emphasis upon the role of reason gave rise to an astonishingly rich body of philosophical work, which is so far little-known in the West. Perhaps the most significant of the great thinkers within the tradition were the Indian masters Dharmakirti and Nagarjuna. The former, through his work on the system of Valid Cognition, established a clear defence of Buddhist doctrines of perception, rebirth and causality, while Nagarjuna, in his Middle Way works, primarily concerned himself with elucidation of the Buddha's teaching on ultimate truth. We will be drawing upon their work at various points in this book.

What is more, unlike systems of mere theory, Buddhism offers a system of contemplative methods through which the essential truth to which it points can be experienced directly. Thus, within the Buddhist tradition, it is not considered sufficient merely to possess the correct theory of the world, since, unless one's actual way of relating to that world is changed, the causes of suffering will still be emotionally operative within us. In other words, the truth about reality must be cultivated or 'brought into being' through 'meditation'. Thus the role of meditation is to cultivate an attention to truth so that it may be experienced at first hand. In so doing, one is, of course, following the example of the Buddha himself, for whom the truth was liberating exactly because he knew it experientially, thus 'awakening' from his bewitchment by erroneous views.

Unlike theism, which commences from an appeal to faith in the authority of revelation, Buddhism asks us to start with a dispassionate examination of our experience, actions and motivations. Of course, for such analysis to be effective, systematic attentiveness is required, which therefore requires us to practise meditation, so that we do not flounder in a mere piling up of ideas about the world rather than unmasking and liberating ourselves from our projections.

Through such attentiveness, founded on the twin contemplative methods of 'calm-abiding' and 'insight', we will be able to scrape away the encrusted fantasies and misconstructions that characterise our present way of relating to the world. Thus, to engage in Buddhist spiritual practice is not a matter of an uncritical acceptance of particular notions about the world but of utilising the guidance left behind by the Buddha in order that we might awaken to the true nature of that world. We will have more to say about this in later chapters.

All other philosophical opinions are characterised by Buddhism as either 'eternalist' or 'annihilationist'. Although these are technical terms drawn from Buddhism, they represent a very useful way of categorising the core beliefs of all non-Buddhist thinkers. In this respect, then, 'eternalist' systems are those philosophies or religions which propose that there are entities which possess permanence. One form of such an opinion would be the belief in a creator god and the immortal souls created by him, as maintained in Christianity, Judaism, Islam and some forms of Hinduism. Another version would be the postulation of a permanent self that dwells within all beings, which is, at the same time, fully identical with the supreme reality itself, as is argued in the Hindu Advaita system. Obviously, however, it was 'eternalist' theories in a Christian form that provided the dominant intellectual assumptions of the West until recent times.

Those opinions that one might label 'annihilationist' are all those theories that argue, by contrast with the 'eternalists', that there can be no past or future lives, because there is no reality to the mind, it being nothing more than physical processes. Thus, according to those theories, at death the body merely returns to the elements and that is the end of life. Such notions were maintained by the Lokayata school[10] over two millennia ago in India and by certain schools of thought in Ancient Greece, and they are held nowadays by the proponents of philosophical materialism whose rise we have briefly surveyed.

Buddhism, for its part, sees both of these types of systems as deviating from a correct perception of the world. Whereas the 'eternalists' distort the continuity and inter-connectedness that are evident in all processes in to a notion of permanence, the 'annihilationists' distort the change and development that are also evident in all processes in to a denial of continuity. The teachings of the Buddha offer a 'Middle Way' that transcends these extremes.

In this respect, as we have mentioned above, the profound nature of Buddha's thought is most fully understood by utilising the insights of the great thinkers such as Nagarjuna, whose Middle Way view dispensed with any belief in permanent entities, while preserving the continuity between actions and results, which continuity is, of course, merely another name for karma.

To be specific, in the Middle Way view, all phenomena are empty of any inherent existence – selfhood, if you like – precisely because they arise through dependence, whether it be dependence upon an assembly of causes and conditions, dependence upon their own constituent parts or dependence upon merely being designated as existent by an observing mind. Thus, emptiness and dependence are the same reality seen from two different sides. The world and the beings within it are not static entities and thus there is both change and continuity interwoven as the very fabric of everything that appears.

What all this means is that Buddhism offers a way out of the chaos that has descended upon Western thought in four particular areas.

First, where the retreat from ideas of God and the soul has fatally undermined the rationale for moral action, since it has dissolved the notion both of a divine authority who will administer reward or punishment, as well as any entity who might receive such, Buddhism provides a sure foundation for it. In other words, while it is non-theistic, Buddhism retains a moral seriousness, since it does not need to invent imaginary static entities, whether souls or gods, to argue for the consequences of actions – consequences which often stretch beyond this very life to ripen at a later moment in the stream of being of which our present human existence is just a temporary manifestation.

Secondly, although Christianity had offered, at least in its more contemplative forms – such as Hesychasm[11] or that of the Rhineland mystics[12] – a species of religious experience, but one tethered to a theism, just as Judaism had done in such systems as the Kabbalah of Isaac Luria (1534–1572),[13] such systems are vulnerable to attack by reasoning, due to their essential theism. Buddhism, by contrast, offers its repertoire of contemplative practices in a non-theistic setting. It is this that renders it an approach to spiritual experience particularly suitable for our somewhat sceptical modern temper.

Thirdly, where scientism claims to represent reason triumphant over religion, Buddhism's philosophical praxis counters this and reinstates human subjectivity and the transcendent without any retreat to blind faith and submission to a divine authority.

Finally, where political ideologies promise a radical transformation of society but can end up delivering enslavement, the Buddha's teaching offers the means, necessarily human-scale, to begin this work in a wiser way by acknowledging that such transformation needs to begin in the intimate sphere of our own heart. We discuss these twin themes in further detail in Chapters 4 and 9.

Therefore, one might say that Buddhism remedies the deficiencies of both Christianity and her rebellious daughters: science and politics. If this is so, its appearance in the West could not be more timely.

Nevertheless, for Buddhism to be effective in this way, the temptation to accommodate it to the ruling ideas of our age must be resisted. After all, it is precisely their insufficiency and their blindness which have created the space for the teachings of the Buddha. This is a theme we will return to in the next two chapters, which will examine Buddhism's relationship to both science and politics: two areas where untutored enthusiasm and an unawareness of underlying assumptions could be somewhat problematic for Buddhism's development in the West.

Chapter 3
Science

Science seems omnipresent in the modern world; its explanatory force and benefits are hard to deny. Indeed, its seemingly unstoppable rise in status, which we touched upon earlier, has led some to argue that Buddhism itself must be made more 'scientific' if it is to survive. We will examine that argument here in this chapter, since it is essential to distinguish 'science' – a means of analysing and describing the world, which is not itself dependent upon any particular philosophical view of the world – from 'scientism', which is an offshoot of the philosophical theory of materialism.

On the face of it, the suggestion to make Buddhism more 'scientific' seems quite compelling. Nevertheless, if we examine the true implications of suggestions such as this, it will become clear that such a project could not really work, and would not be any help, even if it were achievable. It's not, by the way, that one should argue that Buddhism needs to be placed in a special protected category reserved for 'faiths', a reservation into which reasoning is not allowed. In this respect, Buddhism does not resemble the varieties of theism, the authority of which rest (contrary to what Descartes had hoped), in the final analysis, on the acceptance of divine revelation. Rather, it is because the dharma, the body of Buddha's teachings, need only be defended by direct experience and reasoning, and it has no need to borrow these from science. In other words, Buddhism already possesses the reasoning that is needed as a tool to verify and defend its views. Moreover, it seems that those who claim the need for a more 'scientific' Buddhism are perhaps in fact trying to subvert Buddhism to a philosophical belief system disguised as science.

Most of that which is presented as 'science' in these discussions is not actually scientific praxis but a philosophical theory – 'materialism' – and it is essential that we distinguish between the two. Whereas scientific discoveries continue to be made, modern philosophical materialism is, in most important respects, identical to the materialist systems of ancient India, systems which Buddha and the great masters of our tradition knew and rejected. In both its ancient and modern iterations, materialism asserts that consciousness is, at best, merely an epiphenomenon deriving entirely from physical sources ('the four elements', or, nowadays, electrical and chemical processes in the brain). However, in either case, the assertion that sentience as an effect can be conjured from non-sentient causes violates all reasoning. No matter how many electrical or chemical processes there may be, they do not add up to consciousness (the formless continuity that experiences and cognises the world), but only the rearrangement of physical processes. So much, incidentally, for materialism's 'cutting edge' modernity – a notion advanced solely to intimidate us in to thinking that it's the irresistible wave of the future.

In fact, the contemporary insistence that science alone can answer all questions about the nature of reality is actually 'scientism', as we have described it earlier, a type of quasi-religious faith that scientific knowledge is the only knowledge worthy of the name. Most embarrassingly for its proponents, though they keep it well hid, this very belief in science is a premise and not a finding ever arrived at by any type of investigation.

Materialism cannot explain how life arose out of non-life, or how consciousness arose from the non-conscious, with any more compelling seriousness than the theist who declares that God simply said: 'Let there be light.' This modern materialism adds nothing to older materialist theories except the illusion that if complex physical processes are described in minute enough detail, we, the audience, will not notice the sleight of hand involved when sentience is magically conjured out of non-sentient matter – a notion about as plausible as Pinocchio becoming a real boy. The descriptions of how physical processes appear may be valid enough, but inferences from those about how life arose, and the ontological nature of those appearances, are not.

Buddhism has nothing to fear from science, nor, crucially, any need to prostrate to it. It is the proper job of science to formulate and test hypotheses about how physical processes appear to work. Thus science is no doubt unparalleled in detecting and quantifying things that have a material or mechanistic explanation, such as the structure of DNA, but it cannot do any more than that. This inbuilt limitation does not invalidate the usefulness of the scientific enterprise, but it entails that it can have nothing of value to say about such topics as the nature of mind itself. Nor can it add anything of value about the nature of ethical behaviour and altruism, and liberation from the cycle of suffering, which are the core concerns of Buddhism. Of course, science has many valuable things to say about the brain and nervous system, which, from a Buddhist point of view, are the co-operating conditions that must be present for the mind to interact with the world.

While science itself is not dangerous for the Buddha's teaching, what is dangerous is when the call for a 'scientific Buddhism' is actually an insistence that Buddhism must accord with the materialist propositions of 'scientism'. To insist that Buddhism must accord with principles that are, in fact, philosophical tenets of materialism (going beyond the proper scientific praxis of science) would be to contradict the essential philosophical views of Buddhism. Such a Buddhism would be no Buddhism. It would be a shrunken, desiccated apology for Buddhism, denuded of core Buddhist teachings.

A Buddhism refashioned to accommodate materialism would, for instance, necessarily be a Buddhism without rebirth. Thus, if there is no mind but merely material processes, there can be no past and future lives. This would follow, because, once this present body came to an end at death, there could be no further basis for experience.

One might say at this point that the Buddhist teaching of rebirth is too remote from our experience and so we must insist on a new type of Buddhism. Yet, in actuality, rebirth is both extraordinarily simple and a continuous process: we pass away both from moment to moment and life to life. In fact, we can find the profound and thus temporarily hidden truth of rebirth from life to life by seeing the process as it occurs here and now. The more we understand that our nature is one of fluidity, that we are in fact always in the process of being born, the more relaxed we become about the movement from life to life. In short, it is our attachment to the idea of ourselves as a static fixed entity, one bounded around either by God (which is, in general terms, the view of 'theists') or the sleep of non-existence (which is generally the view of 'materialists'), that makes us resist the truth of rebirth, which is, finally, nothing more than the truth that all reality is process – a process in which, ultimately, there are no radical discontinuities.

Incidentally, it is not just the fundamental teaching of rebirth that would be cast out in this 'scientistic' Buddhism: so too would be the related teaching of karma. If the reality of mind is denied, it inevitably follows that it would render redundant any talk about action (karma) and the attendant ripening of deeds, a theory that is key to Buddhist moral thought. According to the Buddha, karma is primarily mental in character. Thus, if one traces the evolution of any particular action, it begins as a mental intention, whether non-virtuous or virtuous – that is to say, contaminated with the poisonous emotions of desire, hatred and ignorance or motivated by their virtuous corollaries. Subsequently, then, this mental action or intention might be translated into a physical or verbal action. However, if one accepts the materialist's ostensible denial of mind – as such a person must want us to do, if he or she is talking in good faith – it makes as little sense to talk of intention or motivation as to ascribe motivation to a vacuum cleaner.

According to Buddhism, our actions shape our future experience primarily through the establishment of tendencies to certain types of experiences and actions. These tendencies are then carried forward in the mindstream, as the thinkers of the 'Mind Only' system of tenets have described, but will only manifest if and when the appropriate supporting conditions are present. Since there is no hidden hand organising things, such as that of God, but only the interaction of the limitless array of phenomena that comprise the world, the time when the fruits of our actions arise may be a very long way in the future. This, in summary, is the meaning of karma – a tragically much mischaracterised and misunderstood doctrine.

If there were really no mind (and perhaps just the electrical and chemical impulses of the brain instead, as the materialists insist) the Buddhist distinction between non-virtue and virtue would also collapse. The distinction between these two is predicated on intention, and, as we have just noted, in the absence of mind, one cannot conceive of intention. Furthermore, since the Buddha's diagnosis of our situation suggests that the immediate and most central cause of the suffering we inflict on ourselves and others is the domination of our actions by the primary emotions of desire, hatred and ignorance, to argue for a world without mind would be utterly contradictory to this analysis. In short, without the mental event of the disturbing emotions, there would be no causes of suffering, let alone any mind to experience them.

One could go on detailing the abolition of all the key teachings of Buddhism that such a 'scientific Buddhism' would entail, but it's easy to see, without looking too far, that this wouldn't leave any Buddhism, except, maybe, sitting cross-legged and talking peaceably about peace. It's possible that this kind of activity makes some kind of commercial sense as the 'Buddhism' sold nowadays at expensive workshops on 'spirituality', but it's not a Buddhism that's ever been known among a single one of our predecessors.

Of course, one accepts that not everyone who discerns an importance in fostering a dialogue between Buddhism and science is an advocate of such a 'non-Buddhist Buddhism'. Indeed, there can be certain scientific analyses, most obviously in fields like physics, where some researchers are ineluctably drawn to find resonances with such Buddhist teachings as the interdependence and emptiness of phenomena. In such cases, it is easy enough to accept that such people might well be inspired by Buddhism after studying such disciplines.

Nevertheless, in too many instances, one cannot help but notice that many of those from the Buddhist side of any putative dialogue with scientists are unqualified to distinguish between actual scientific praxis and scientism, and between legitimate scientific work and the bogus philosophical claims that may be smuggled in to such discussion by mislabelling them 'science'. Unfortunately, they are often unaware that, in Buddhist terms, science is not a 'view' – defined in Buddhism as being a total way of understanding the nature of reality, as is the case with a philosophy or religious system – because scientific praxis is distinct from any philosophy or religious system. Consequently, they mistakenly believe that all scientific practitioners subscribe to a monolithic world view.

Furthermore, even when such misunderstandings are overcome, one is still entitled to wonder what the utility of much of this dialogue might be, when one notes, for instance, the emphasis placed, in such meetings between Buddhists and scientists, on such philosophically trivial matters as validating meditation practice by the study of brainwaves during meditation. Of course, one may concede, for the sake of argument, that brain activity might change during meditation, but it remains difficult to see how this knowledge could contribute anything significant to the process of dissolving the twin obscurations of disturbing emotions and ignorance, a dissolution that alone will bring about enlightenment. Would, for instance, Jetsun Milarepa (1040–1123), the most eminent yogin of the Kagyu tradition, have achieved decisive realisation more swiftly if he had possessed a knowledge of neurology? The question needs only to be raised to be answered. The plain truth is that a variety of physical effects, from the modification of the pulse rate to altered frequency of brainwaves, may accompany meditation, but these effects are not the primary source of the experience of the meditating mind any more than a lessening of indigestion during meditation would be.

In short, even this understandable wish to advance Buddhism by linking it with the prestige of science might sometimes obscure the actual power of Buddhism. The unique force of the Buddha's teachings lies in its diagnosis of suffering and its causes, and its prescription of the path to the cessation of that suffering. This fact alone means that Buddhism can speak for itself, even in the modern marketplace of ideas. It follows from this that the best way we can help preserve the Buddha's teaching is to stay true to it. Right about now, that might be the most radical thing to do.

Chapter 4
Politics

The teachings of the Buddha offer us a means of revising our understanding of who we are and what is the nature of the world. Inevitably, such a revision must lead to a shift in our way of engaging with others. After all, it is undeniable that a key dictum of the Buddhist teachings is the motif of interdependence, where nothing and nobody truly exists in isolation. Thus, if we change ourselves, we begin to change the world. So, as this is the case, what follows in this chapter is not a piece of advocacy for a total disengagement.

Nevertheless, it seems that there is a pressing need to avoid the subjection of the spiritual life to politics. In our particular case as Buddhists, it is a matter of preserving a space in which the liberating force of Buddhism can work. When we make this argument, we are not insisting that we must avoid each and every social responsibility, just as we are not seeking to deny the usefulness of science when we argue that Buddhism should resist the siren call of scientism. However, it is to say that there is an urgent need to rebalance the relationship between religion ('spirituality', if you insist) and politics, at a time, and in a culture, when the prestige and power of politics has increased alarmingly, and that of religion has almost entirely faded away.

Any dispassionate observation of the modern scene can lead only to the melancholy conclusion that the greater our obsession with politics and political ideology, the more

29

territory they appear to occupy in our lives. Political ideology is, to quote a phrase, 'a jealous god'. It doesn't want any competitors for our allegiance. That is why it will chase the spiritual dimension from our lives and our society unless we resist it.

A clear and present danger exists for Buddhism in the West at the current time. As has happened before in its history, it could easily be made subservient to political ideology. Whereas, for instance, in Japan in the 1930s and 1940s some elements of Zen Buddhism were made accomplice to chauvinistic militarism,[14] here it appears that another type of subversion of Buddhism may be at work. I refer to the soft but possibly lethal subversion that is evident in the accommodation, or perhaps capitulation, of Buddhism, in the USA and other places, to a package of fashionable and 'progressive' notions, some of which may be benign, but some of which clearly contradict Buddhist views concerning the beginning and end of life and the practice of non-violence.

Although there is, in such areas, a sharp distinction between authentically Buddhist values and those of contemporary society, a troublingly large proportion of Western Buddhists seem not to have noticed this. As a result, they unquestioningly accept our dominant political and ethical paradigms. Anyone who needs any confirmation of this last point need only look at the major Buddhist journals on sale today or visit most Buddhist centres attended by Westerners. I have even heard some individuals, who are known as teachers in the USA, declare that Buddha's account of suffering is incomplete and that its deficiencies must be made up for by accepting the superior analyses proffered by political ideology. While one might expect this from a non-Buddhist, one has to ask how such a person can take themselves seriously as a Buddhist, let alone as a teacher of Buddhism. In fact, Buddha's teachings provide a comprehensive account of suffering and its antidote. To deny this fact is to deny the effectiveness of the path taught by the Buddha himself.

Unhappily, few of the Western converts to Buddhism who read these publications or visit these centres seem to have given any thought to the logical consequences of holding the erroneous view that Buddha's teachings are deficient and must be supplemented by political ideology. However, the sad fate of the mainline Christian churches should serve as a warning as to how subverting traditional religious teachings to fashionable ideology can destroy a once-great spiritual tradition. The embrace of secular political views by these churches and their attempts to be more attractive by shedding traditional forms and doctrines have led to the evisceration of their spiritual seriousness and all but guaranteed their demise. Their decline is a sad testimony as to what happens when we seek to please the crowd by subordinating our teaching to political and modish causes.

In comparison to the lingering sense of death that thus surrounds much mainstream Christianity, Buddhism still has a somewhat vigorous spiritual life. The fact that the essence of Buddha's teachings is still flourishing is just as it should be, for these teachings are a radically distinctive system of philosophical analysis and contemplative practice, a system which points beyond the accidents of culture, beyond even birth and death themselves, to the fundamental ground of reality. However, there is now a strong possibility that what is sold, packaged and described as 'Buddhism' will become nothing more than an 'add-on' for those whose deepest apprehensions and values are not Buddhist at all but who merely desire the scent of an unthreatening 'spirituality' to fill out their identity.

In order to reaffirm the primacy of Buddha's teaching over worldly systems and opinions, we modern Buddhists must avoid the error of tying it to any particular transient political ideology, old or new and wherever it may be located on the political spectrum. For one thing, doing so inevitably discourages people with divergent opinions from attending Buddhist events, whereas one might expect that the universal appeal of Buddha's teachings would mean that those of a huge range of differing opinions would wish to attend. If we seek to tie Buddhism exclusively to any particular political beliefs, Buddhist communities will then become culturally and intellectually monochrome, and, finally, fade into irrelevance when the cultural fashions move on. In the end, however, the key point is that no such ideology can represent Buddhism, because inevitably it will possess neither its depth nor its vastness. Any ideology can only shrink, if not actually distort, the teachings of the Buddha. Thus, as should be obvious, Buddhism belongs neither to the left nor right nor centre.

At this point, some might argue that, contrary to what I have said above, it is easy to equate the Buddha's teaching with a particular form of politics. For instance, they might claim that a political ideology can be found in Buddha's teaching that is identical with a particular modern political platform. However, it would be useful for them to remember that Buddha himself counselled both monarchs and the Shakyan 'republic' during his lifetime. Hence it is not obvious which particular form of state governance he might have preferred. Historically speaking, Buddhist polities have principally been monarchical, with sometimes happy and sometimes unhappy results, and, although various monarchies have drawn on Buddhist symbolism and prior history to embellish and underpin their rule, it is not difficult to imagine other forms of governance doing the same.

Nor is there necessarily any ideal form of economic arrangement that can be adduced from Buddha's teachings, beyond the need for honesty and the repudiation of theft in one's dealings with others. The Buddha's teachings themselves spread rapidly during the Buddha's lifetime within the newly urbanised and entrepreneurial economies of fifth-century BCE northern India, and Buddha received extensive support from the upwardly mobile merchant class. Thus, although Buddha counselled against greed, which is an obstacle to spiritual practice, he did not discourage prudent accumulation of wealth by his lay followers, which, in the absence of greed, can be very helpful in enabling one to undertake and support spiritual practice and charitable endeavours. Equally, later on, Buddhism became, in various places, a religion of agrarian peasantry, of nomadic pastoralists and of urban intellectuals, all with their varying social and economic structures. Thus, we cannot extrapolate much of an economic ideology from the variety of economic structures in which Buddha's teachings flourished both during his lifetime and after his death.

Conceding all this, some might still opine that, to give a voice to Buddhism in the modern world, it is, all the same, important to fashion a political movement that will best represent it. For instance, we might set about disseminating a Buddhist political ideology so that Buddhists could form a voting bloc, and, perhaps, even a Buddhist political party, which would (more peacefully and more mindfully than our political opponents, of course) gradually assume power. Although opinions on the desirability of such a development may differ, it might be as well to admit that the history of partisanship exercised by Buddhist religious governments or parties is not very encouraging, even, it must be admitted, in Tibet.[15]

For us Buddhists, the most important of all questions are: 'What is the source of suffering, and what is to be done about it?' Incidentally, one must notice right away that the 'suffering' referred to here is not merely the discontents and miseries of this life, but, from the Buddhist point of view, also the sufferings of death and what follows, since each life is played out within the continuity of repeated birth and death until liberation is gained. Thus, as for followers of Christianity and Judaism, there is, for the followers of the Buddha, a cosmic dimension to suffering.

While religions, in their differing ways, insist upon the cosmic and interior dimensions of suffering, these dimensions are entirely absent in the account of suffering and the remedies proposed for it in modern political ideologies. Such ideologies, whether Marxist, anarchist, National Socialist, fascist, libertarian or ecological – in short, whatever position they occupy on the so-called political map – locate the primary source of ill in external conditions, and, by the by, either entirely or at least partially, exclude or deny any reference to a future life. As Rousseau, the grandfather of most modern political ideology, put it: 'Man is born free but is everywhere in chains.'[16] Hence, thinkers in this line claim that, by transforming these external conditions through social change, the desired state of happiness will be obtained. In later iterations of this creed, the power of both science and technology to effect change has been added to the struggle to create a perfect world. As Lenin said: 'Soviet power plus electrification equals communism.'[17]

The first problem with these ideologies is their materialist reduction of the human to a merely physical being, for whom a mere arrangement of physical circumstances can bring about the abolition of suffering. Hence the ideologue ignores the mind, and, with it, the very messiness and complexity of the causes of suffering, which no external rearrangement will change.

A second flaw in these ideological schemes is that, as we have mentioned earlier, they depend, bizarrely enough, upon an acceptance of a myth of progress derived from the Christian notion of history as a linear progression. Simply put, it is not difficult to discern the Christian intellectual substructure in the historical orientation shared by these ideologies.

This embarrassing and thus unacknowledged borrowing is evident in the manner in which such ideologies all invoke a pre-lapsarian state of perfection, albeit with the Garden of Eden now recast as Rousseau's 'state of nature', the Marxist 'primitive communism' and so on, which is then lost through original sin in the form of laws and private property, which deformities culminate in the sufferings experienced through capitalism, until, finally, in the end of days, there will be the Second Coming and the attendant end of history, now reconfigured, for instance, as the Revolution and the triumph of the proletariat, or whichever is the oppressed group *de nos jours*.

Of course, a slightly variant version was proffered after the collapse of Communism by some American thinkers such as Francis Fukuyama, where history ends with the triumph of American liberal democracy and capitalism.[18] In any event, how amusing it is that all these avowedly anti-Christian movements are recycling the Christian vision of history, and, just like the hapless millenarians of the past, have to fall back on ever more desperate excuses as to why the promised utopia never turns up. In short, these political ideologies, with their promise of a perfect society and a perfected human being, are selling old-time fairy tales in modern clothing. There is not a shred of evidence for the truth of the promises that are being made. If one does want to accept these doctrines, one must make a leap of faith much more strenuous than that required of the Christian believer. To borrow from the great Oscar Wilde slightly – one would have to possess a heart of stone not to laugh at the mental contortion required of such political votaries.

A third failing of political ideologies, as we noted in passing earlier, is that they so often serve as a convenient way to hide from one's own inner disturbing emotions and moral failings and to project these upon others. All too frequently, ideology and politics are greed, hatred and delusion in action. As the bard from Minnesota has declared:

Power and greed and corruptible seed
Seem to be all that there is.[19]

This is evident in the manner in which politics always plays off one against another. Here is Bob Dylan again, musing (and amusing) this time on the ideologues involved in the shipwreck of contemporary culture:

Praise be to Nero's Neptune.
The Titanic sails at dawn.
Everybody is shouting 'Which side are you on?'[20]

In fact, the divisiveness inherent in ideology tends to suggest that it might sometimes be attractive precisely because the excitement and pleasures of hatred that it engenders can be more compelling than any wish to render help to others. The pleasurable frisson in the conviction of what a good person one is being in following such ideologies only adds to the heady mix. One might even wonder if it is not the case that the real satisfaction for most successful ideologues is actually the coercion and manipulation of others. Nowadays, and coincident with the decline of religion, this coercion would most likely be clothed in some talk of 'compassion', borrowed (or perhaps that should be 'appropriated') from an enfeebled Christianity or an undemanding, and hence 'acceptable', Buddhism.

Thus, whereas most religions require that people must improve internally and morally, and accordingly generally maintain a certain realism and patience about the speed of such transformation (over a period of one or a number of lives), political ideology, acknowledging no inner life and no future lives, demands immediate obedience. It is thus willing to punish ideological non-conformity severely. It categorises people into sinner and saved – now re-christened 'correct' and 'incorrect' – just as swiftly and confidently as any old-time Puritan preacher. It polices all signs and manifestations of ideological non-conformity with the zeal of any Inquisitor.

The state of perfection that is chased by political ideologies is, of course, unattainable. Like any other object of desire, it is merely a projection of mind's disturbing emotions. Thus, as with drinking salt water to assuage thirst, so the achieving of any desired political, cultural or social objectives by these ideologues is never satisfying enough for them. Hence, it must be followed by a new objective to be fulfilled. So the ratchet tightens, as it must forever, and with it the past is abolished, since remembrance of what had gone before would betray the fact that what was advertised as the state of perfection that would bring about the final end of all activity has turned out not to be the final end.

Hence those who were once revolutionary must either upgrade ('evolve') their views and objectives, or be consumed by the ravenous demands of progress and its new exigencies. Indeed, the demand for ever-greater political purity increases as the parsing of an ever-greater refinement of objectives grows. In this way, Robespierre cannot but fall victim to the next round of purges. Incidentally, religious communities – including Buddhists – who assure themselves that they will never fall victim to the intolerance of the ideologue who seeks to prevent them from practising their religion should perhaps re-think their assumptions. Their day will come.

Thus, for many, including a disturbingly large contingent of people who consider themselves to be Buddhists, modern political ideology has come, sometimes perhaps even unwittingly, to be a substitute religion. In other words, it is the source of their most deeply felt values. Tragically, however, such political ideology is, in many respects, simply the expression of a decayed and borrowed fantasy exercised largely by the morally delinquent. Such ideologues, once in power, can then induce the people to support them by pandering to their basest instincts – greed, hatred and delusion (the 'three poisons'), which are, according to Buddha, the actual roots of our discontent.

Concerning rulers, Ezra Pound's lines seem apt:

All men, in law, are equals.
. . . . [but]
We choose a knave or an eunuch
To rule over us.[21]

According to Buddhism, the route to freedom from suffering lies not through such manipulation of the external world but through inner reform: a transformation in our understanding, experience and actions. Thus, if one reposes the question asked earlier concerning the source of suffering, our answer will be that it flows directly from our choices to act in a self-centred way. As regards those choices, whichever ones are made under the influence of desire, hatred and ignorance are, *ipso facto*, non-virtuous and thus can only bring about suffering for ourselves and others, even if that suffering is not immediately apparent.

The inevitable link between selfish behaviour and consequent suffering is that they are rooted in a mistaken notion of ourselves and the world: one that assumes that we ourselves possess an identity contiguous with our body or mind that is permanent, singular and autonomous (whether we call it 'a self', a 'personality' or something else) and that phenomena 'out there in the world', likewise possessing the characteristics of solidity, can be appropriated or rejected, bent to our will. In short, we are in conflict with reality, and, consequently, none of our endeavours can bring authentic freedom from suffering. On the contrary, further suffering is ensured as each repeated round of disappointment, frustration and misery merely fires up another doomed attempt to wrest happiness from a world uncontrollable by our ego.

Thus the definitive source of suffering, rather than being external, lies in mind. Yet it is not that mind itself is some truly existent thing that is inherently impure or irretrievably wicked, or, on the contrary, inherently good. It is presently covered by the veils of unawareness and disturbing emotions, but, through the process of study, reflection and meditation (the three trainings that constitute the work of inner reform), it can be freed from these obscurations. With such liberation, one's capacity for wisdom and compassion, from which we are alienated in our present self-centred state, will irradiate our life and that of others. Such is the meaning of being a Buddha. Such unceasing concern and work for others is what a Buddha does. Such a truly radical state is, contrary to certain modern watered-down interpretations, the meaning of enlightenment.

Furthermore, in absolute contrast to modern political ideologies, with their notion of ineluctable and irreversible progress, Buddhism sees impermanence and change as inevitable for all that is created. Thus no final perfect state of society can be attained. No kingdoms nor republics, no nations nor civilisations can endure forever, no more than our body, relationships, status or opinions. All such things rise, and, in time, fall, as all arise from the nexus of causes and conditions. Ameliorations in external conditions, economic or social, are certainly not impossible but are always, at best, provisional and temporary.

Additionally, it is hard to have much enthusiasm for the proposition that politicians should be trusted to bring about the betterment of humankind, as political ideology insists. Outside the state of spiritual perfection which is Buddhahood, the contamination of motives and actions by moral and philosophical selfishness is unavoidable. To ignore this sober estimate of our actual current state, and to imagine that people such as ourselves – for let us not forget that politicians and ideologues are people such as ourselves – can engineer happiness, simply through rearranging the external world, is fanciful indeed. Perhaps, in entrusting the world to them, we are, in a peculiar way, asking too much of them.

The crux of the matter is this: from a Buddhist perspective, nirvana alone is true freedom from suffering, since it is the extinction of the fires of the ignorance and disturbing emotions that are the very source of suffering. These causes of misery have not arisen randomly in this life, but, as we noted in Chapter 2, out of our profound misunderstanding concerning the nature of things, which sets us at odds with the world. Consequently, their dissolution can only occur through encountering emptiness, the unproduced and unceasing nature of reality that is, simultaneously, our own true nature. Thus, there is, at the heart of Buddhism, a space that is unending and unlimited, that transcends history, language, culture and society. Is it even necessary to add that it also transcends politics?

Thus, for Buddhism, an 'inner reform' is necessary, yet, as in the example of Buddha's own life, it is a reform that will blossom outward in engagement with others. Incidentally, in citing the Buddha's example, one must not conclude that working for the welfare of others must wait until enlightenment has been attained. In fact, working for others is also a fundamental part of the path to enlightenment.

In short, the development of wisdom and compassion forms the core of the process of spiritual development. Between these two, there is a relationship of reciprocity, as each aids the growth of the other. However, it would be unhelpful to interpret the need for working for others to develop wisdom and compassion as meaning an insistence on political involvement as we define it nowadays, that is to say, crudely put, supporting or participating in an ideologically-driven mass movement that wishes to shape and control society, as those modern Buddhists who have unthinkingly bought the 'package' of progressive opinions believe.

So, that being the case, how should we begin to engage with the world?

The answer, in a word, is 'carefully'. It should be obvious that, as beginners, given that we are influenced so strongly by our unruly emotions and the imprints of our past choices and actions, there is a need for thoughtfulness and modesty in our behaviour. The necessity of these qualities is a major concern of the teaching on ethics presented by Buddha and the great masters of our tradition. In passing, we can concede that much of what is taught on such matters in Buddhism is itself consistent with the moral intuitions and prescriptions transmitted throughout the generations of human culture, inside and outside of Buddhism itself.

In contrast to this acknowledgement of the value of transmitted wisdom, a particularly insistent theme in modern culture – originating, perhaps, in a 'polyamorous' union of Marx, Freud and Rousseau – has been that we need to free ourselves from the burden of tradition and religious teaching and act spontaneously in a manner that is 'true to ourselves'. However, from a Buddhist point of view, this makes little sense. As we have seen, the notion that one can isolate a unique, autonomous self to which we could 'be true' is profoundly mistaken. To say, as Buddha did, that we exist only through interdependence is to say that we exist within a framework of reciprocal duties and responsibilities, and, equally, within the historical continuity of those who have gone before us. If we are to nurture wisdom and compassion, if we are truly to achieve freedom, and if we are to bring benefit to others, we must start with this sense of connectedness: one that is expressed in the fundamental ethical precept of not harming others (and, furthermore, not harming oneself, since actions that harm oneself reduce one's capacity to benefit others).

There is also a modesty in the manner in which Buddhist moral training commences with the local and the particular. For example, the traditional instructions for the meditative cultivation of altruism usually begin with thinking of one's family in the love of a child for parents and in the love of a parent for his or her child. It then is widened outwards by 'bringing' the more distant in to the ambit of one's love, thus enlarging one's family, so to speak, until it is truly universal. However, even here, we are far from the mass movement or the ideologue, who, sadly, so often loves humankind in the abstract but is repelled by the actual individual human. We will return to this point in a later chapter.

The 'personalism' of the Buddhist approach to working for others stands in some contrast to the behaviour of the ideologue. In Buddhism, one is personally required to engage in giving and so on, whereas, as is all too common with the ideologically inclined, their spirit of generosity is signified by the demand that somebody else actually bear the cost of the giving they advocate, perhaps through the government or some other agency redistributing the wealth of others. It's a personally cost-free way of giving.

Despite the radical demand of the Buddhist ethic that we must engage with the world in a truly altruistic way without any trace of self-clinging, it is, as we have stressed above, this person, this being or these beings to whom one responds. Thus it is never programmatic but always person-centred, in the spirit of Dylan's beautiful line:

> If you see your neighbour carrying something, help him with his load.[22]

What, then, of political involvement?

As we noted earlier, Buddha himself counselled political rulers during his lifetime, and we can also cite the examples of Sakya Pandita and his nephew Chogyal Phakpa in thirteenth-century Tibet. Both of these masters of the Sakya school acted as preceptors of Mongol rulers. Sakya Pandita was able to mitigate much of the ferocity of Prince Godan by dissuading him from the mass murder of his Chinese subjects.[23] Some years later, Chogyal Phakpa was able to prevent Kublai Khan from imposing religious conformity upon the empire, even though it would have benefited Chogyal Phakpa's own tradition.[24]

Few of us will be in such an exalted and influential position, and perhaps we should reflect occasionally on the tremendous burden the morally upright person in authority has taken on. In such cases, gratitude towards them is merited. Sometimes, however, it can seem that the best we can hope for from political arrangements is to be able to find and preserve the space for Buddhist teaching and practice. Indeed, there might be times when we Buddhists will consider that all that we can do is pray to the female bodhisattva Tara, traditionally held to bestow succour on the afflicted, for protection from the punishments that politicians so often mete out to their helpless subjects.

In any event, what should be clear is that Buddha's teachings do not traffic in illusions, utopian or otherwise. They privilege no one above another, as they are not based on the idea of 'self against other' or 'us against them'. They do not dislocate the present from the past or the future, because all three aspects of time are woven together in the continuity of life. They proclaim that all beings are to be cherished throughout their lives, as each being cherishes his or her own life.

Furthermore, since all beings wish for happiness and freedom from suffering just as intently as we do, we should strive to help them grow in virtue now. Only this will create the basis for future happiness. We should also wish for them to have the means to train in the profound topics of the spiritual path, and, in such a way, come to achieve liberation from the cycle of birth and death.

Thus, if we must engage in the political world, we should do so in a manner that is consonant with the demands of these Buddhist ethical injunctions – ethics that come from a vision of the world that is utterly indifferent to the clamour of contemporary ideology.

So perhaps we should forget the slick Men of Peace and the Politics of Peace so valorised in contemporary culture. There can't be any peace until we forgive those who trespass most intimately against us and stop pretending to forgiveness by political gestures and observances. There can't be any peace until we abandon our resentment of those who are more successful, and stop pretending that our anger is compassion. There can't be any peace until we dissolve the enemies in our own heart and stop looking for them in the world. In other words, it is the human heart that has to change in a fundamental way, and no organisation or political movement ever achieved that. For that, we need some teachings that seem to have been long abandoned: 'Give victory to others and take defeat upon yourself.'

Chapter 5
Conceit

There's an old story about a frog. He's lived all his life in a well, but one day another frog appears at the top of the well. They get talking and the strange frog tells the old one that he's come from somewhere called 'the Ocean'.

'I've never heard of that. I guess it's about a quarter of the size of my well?'

'No! More than that!' answers the other.

'OK – a half?'

'Much bigger!' the strange frog laughs.

'The same size, then?'

'No, even bigger!' says the foreign frog.

'Alright. This I need to see!' says the old frog, and he clambers excitedly, despite himself, out of his well and sets off for the ocean.

It's a hard road, but, at last, he arrives there by the ocean side.

Unfortunately, when he finally sees how big it is, the shock is so great that his head explodes.

Lately it occurs to me that this well-loved story told by Patrul Rinpoche, a great nineteenth-century master of the Nyingma tradition, could apply to many of us in our encounter with Buddhism. Just like that frog, we have a bad case of the disease of conceit. We are so confident in the opinions that we bring with us to this encounter that we have no inkling of the vastness of the Buddha's teaching nor how

radically different it is from our preconceptions. In other words, we are the frog before he even gets out of the well.

Such pride is usually characterised as one of the 'six stains' that should be avoided when we receive the teachings.[25] Unfortunately, as Patrul Rinpoche himself pointed out, it is very difficult to recognise it for what it is. However, unless we can dissolve it, our receipt of spiritual teachings will be profitless at best and, at worst, poisonous.

There's something essentially closed-minded about pride. What we need instead is a sense of humility which will render us open to the teachings. The traditional analogy employed for this positive approach to them is that of a vessel placed the right way up so that it can be filled with water. This receptivity is, however, not to be confused with credulity nor a hurried and irritable reaching after certainty when the teachings are difficult. It is, rather, a readiness to attend to the words and meaning of the teaching and then to persist in critical reflection until it has been digested and become a part of our thinking.

Sadly, many of us nowadays believe that we already know all there is to know about Buddhism. Such presumption has a number of causes, but chief among them is the conviction that Buddhism and our own pre-existing assumptions are identical. It seems that this belief is particularly pernicious because it blocks any genuine encounter with the dharma. Perhaps we can represent this belief in the form of a faulty syllogism:

> My opinions are compassionate. Buddhism is compassionate. Therefore Buddhism must be identical with my opinions.

Incidentally, perhaps we are exhibiting a similar lack of self-awareness when we assert that our version of Buddhism is free of dogma. Let me rephrase this in line with what we really mean when we say this:

> Buddhism should be free of dogma (that I don't like). However, Buddhism must conform to contemporary opinions (because they are not dogma and I like them).

In fact, we have to suspend the entirety of our prior assumptions, whether they are religious, political or cultural, if we are going to make the journey with the Buddha to uncover the true nature of reality.

I know this from my own experience. When I met my principal teachers in the early 1970s, I had just departed the 'counter-culture' and I simply assumed that, apart from the issue of drugs, Tibetan masters would subscribe totally to the values of that world. I was astonished to discover that, without exhibiting any rancorous ideology, both my lamas approved of monarchy, something I had scorned as an illusion. From this and other revelations of how Buddhism actually differed wildly from what I had assumed, I began to understand that what is important is not whether a Buddhist should support monarchy but that we have to lay aside our opinions in order to be able to 'listen' without prejudice to what the teaching actually says.

There are many important examples of our casually arrogant habit of assuming, without evidence, that two-and-a-half thousand years of Buddhist teachings are identical to modern opinions or can be made identical with them, as we have seen in the preceding two chapters, which focused on confusions about science and politics. You can see its effect in the dismay expressed by some when they discover traditional Buddhist views on ethical issues to do, for instance, with matters of life and death such as abortion, which, being the deliberate taking of life, is regarded as a very grave moral fault.[26] Often all that results is a determined effort to excise the offending teaching, perhaps in the name of a 'higher compassion', or to re-jig it so that it's fit for this week's fashionable notions. However, in the final end, the embodiment of the timeless truths discovered by the Buddha, his teaching, must take precedence over the disposable opinions of those who worship only the ephemeral, whether it is called 'left' or 'right', 'progressive' or 'conservative', or something else.

One could well guess that our disregard for the actual teaching of Buddhism is one reason why many Asian Buddhists have come to regard Western Buddhists as ultimately unserious. In particular, this might sometimes tempt educated yet more cynical teachers to steer clear of mentioning anything that might challenge and provoke their putative disciples' displeasure. Some such teachers might even decide to alter the teachings themselves lest their sponsors withdraw support. Naturally, such evasiveness would accomplish little for the survival of Buddhism. After all, one might wonder what could be the utility of a dharma that does not undermine our assumptions.

What compounds these problems is that, although Buddhism has sometimes been a minority culture in a surrounding sea of non-Buddhism, its present situation, one where religion itself exists only on the barely tolerated margins, is unprecedented. Thus the contrast between Buddhism in its various Asian forms and how it is situated in this new Western environment is striking. Consider the difference between the position in which, for instance, Tibetan Buddhism presently finds itself in the typically small Western 'dharma centre' attended by a relatively small number of people, in contrast to its former dominant place in the social and cultural continuities of Tibet with enormous monasteries and influence. The gap could hardly be greater. Thus it would appear that Buddha's teaching is at a severe disadvantage nowadays in its power to influence our society and culture.

Perhaps that's why I often hear people arguing that Buddhism has to change to fit in with these modern times, such as by, for instance, excising monasticism and formulating an entirely lay form of the religion. However, I'm not sure what Buddhism they are talking about, as a Buddhism entirely devoid of monasticism is one in which one of its fundamental pillars is missing. In actuality, this whole talk of change versus stasis is misconceived. The accumulated wisdom of the Buddha's tradition has always been transmitted in a living form – from person to person – and thus it is an error to regard it as merely a static body of knowledge. Each link in the chain of the tradition has to re-present the teachings in the light of their own cultural and social setting. We can see this process at work in the early history of Buddhism in Tibet. At that time, the early Tibetan scholars and practitioners worked with their Indian mentors to establish the lines of Indian Buddhist teaching in their new setting – a setting a world away from the intellectually and artistically sophisticated milieu of mediaeval India. Out of this grew the four most influential schools of Tibetan Buddhism – Nyingma, Sakya, Kagyu and Geluk – each with their repertoire of teachings in the form of monastic ordination, bodhisattva vow, and the initiations, transmissions and instructions of 'The Vajra Vehicle'.

However, to accept the necessity of creative re-presentation of the tradition to meet the challenges of new cultures is not at all to believe that we can and should improve upon the essentials of the Buddhist teachings themselves. I believe that such a presumption is prevalent in contemporary Western Buddhist circles as a result of the unacknowledged influence of the idea of progress, which we have discussed in the preceding chapters. The power of this myth is at work whenever people talk of such things as 'what the modern world can do for Buddhism' or 'what must be added to (or deleted from) Buddha's teachings to make them acceptable today'.

As we have indicated earlier, the notion that history is progressive and that, consequently, we are, in important respects, superior to preceding generations, is deeply engrained in our Western habits of thought. Consequently, most of us blithely assume that we are the cleverest humans to appear upon this earth, when the truth is very different. In actuality, for every temporary improvement in one area of human affairs, we can usually point to a corresponding shrinkage of our moral, intellectual or spiritual capacities in another. The record of the twentieth century – one shaped, incidentally, by those who asserted most strongly that history was approaching a perfect climax, whether the Communist state or the Thousand-Year Reich – must be one of the bloodiest in world history. Think of the Shoah or consider the many millions who perished at the hands of Stalin or Mao.

Buddhism, in contrast to the unquestioning optimism of progress, has ideas contrary to all that. It teaches us that history is essentially cyclical, just as nature itself suggests. Therefore societies and civilisations rise and fall, and any progress that may occur is merely temporary. As Vasubandhu says in *The Treasury of Abhidharma*:

> The palaces of impermanence arise and decay, together
> with their inhabitants.[27]

Of course, in any society, certain ideas and social forms possess such a force that they exert a significant influence for a period of time, but, eventually, their energy is exhausted and their influence disappears. We can also acknowledge that some of the cultural patterns of one civilisation may be superior to another – for instance, the Christian emphasis on charity is clearly more benign than the Aztec predilection for human sacrifice, but, in time, however positive or great a civilisation is, all ideologies wither and die.

The fact is, therefore, that if we put aside our conceit and listen carefully to what Buddhism teaches, we will realise that progress is not inevitable. The only lasting change is that which is won by the individual effort to apply the teachings of the Buddha, and, by so doing, finally attain the state of being a Buddha, fully awakened to the nature of reality and endowed with the qualities of wisdom and compassion that flow from the ending of the sleep of ignorance. In this light, it makes no sense to talk and act as if we moderns can improve on the Buddha in respect of moral sensibility, contemplative experience or philosophical insight, among many other items.

We can understand this point by considering the act of 'Taking Refuge', which is the ceremony that traditionally marks one as a Buddhist. In this ceremony one affirms that, from now on, in all one's spiritual endeavours, one will rely upon the Buddha, his teaching and the community of those who practise the Buddha's teaching. To put it plainly, we take refuge in the Buddha because, as the ritual of refuge declares, 'he is best among all humans', since he has realised the true nature of reality. That nature, the emptiness that characterises all phenomena, does not alter: it neither declines nor improves. Consequently, the wisdom that apprehends it cannot be improved upon either. If such were possible, Buddha would not be the Enlightened One and a valid object upon whom we can rely.

As Sakya Pandita cautioned his fellow Tibetans when similar questions of adaptation were a matter of intense debate in the thirteenth century:

One should hold correctly
To the key points of the teaching

Undiluted and in agreement with the sutras and tantras,
For no matter how fine its wheels may be,
A chariot cannot move if its axle is broken,
And the other senses cannot work
If the life faculty has ceased.
Just so, no matter how good other instructions may be,
They are powerless if the key points of the teaching have
    been spoiled.[28]

Thus, when we talk about a (wholly appropriate) adaptation and flexibility, we should avoid confusing this with the notion of improving the Buddha's teachings. None of the intellectual products of our particular civilisation, whether political ideologies or pragmatically useful but ever-revisable scientific hypotheses regarding material processes, possess anything that could improve the core of Buddha's teachings.

So, what is to be done about our conceit? Patrul Rinpoche puts it like this:

See the teaching as the medicine,
Yourself as a sick person,
The teacher as a skilled doctor
And dedicated practice as the cure.[29]

As for the teacher – there are enough genuine ones. If we go and find one, things could start to get interesting for the frog right about now. However, he needs to be careful.

Chapter 6
Disillusionment

It seems like there's a lot of people with some big expectations about Buddhism. At the same time, it seems that there's a whole lot of people who are disappointed with it. Unfortunately, that disappointment all too frequently becomes resentment, and, whereas disappointment can be the first step to wisdom, resentment brings only disaster.

It is a great tragedy that nowadays many people's connection with Buddhism bears all the tell-tale signs of a journey from credulous enthusiasm to resentment. Maybe in some cases it's because they have embraced a phantom – a version of Buddhism that would be unrecognisable to any of our Buddhist predecessors, not to mention the Asian people who still make up the bulk of practising Buddhists – and one, sadly, that cannot benefit them in any profound manner. One need only glance, as we have in the preceding chapters, at the concerns and assumptions of vocal 'Buddhists' in the West to sense that these are two very different worlds, and to wonder what 'Buddhism' it might be that most Westerners have embraced.

In fact, the answer is clear. They have embraced a Buddhism largely of their own projections, albeit in some cases with some skilful prompting by the kind of Asian or Western teachers who are active in the spiritual marketplace. It is a Buddhism shorn of anything objectionable to the upscale inhabitants of London, Santa Monica and Manhattan. It's a

'Buddhism' in which the moral seriousness of traditional Buddhism, a seriousness grounded in respect for others, has been amputated. In its place has been grafted the licence of absolute autonomy to the self, for whom individual choice is the only arbiter of good and evil. In short, rather than abandoning self-centredness (and the other powerful gods of our age) and turning instead to Buddhism, we have found, or so we think, a religion that can accommodate them.

In other words, it is the apparently unthreatening nature of Buddhism that makes it so attractive to those for whom Christian consolations are unfashionable and restrictive. The sophisticated, well-heeled and well-connected are excited to be the guests of honour at the Buddhist party today because they imagine that it demands nothing of them, but I don't see much room for the ordinary, unshowy man or woman with their dirty hands and struggles.

Such a toothless Buddhism, which is only attractive because it is not Christianity, can do nothing to liberate us from the suffering of birth, old age, sickness and death, for it leaves intact the entire machinery of self-clinging, self-cherishing and the ensuing disturbing emotions, and here is the root of the disillusionment many come to experience so often. Such a diluted Buddhism cannot provide support and clarity when difficulties turn up, as difficulties inevitably do, and so those who become disillusioned will either return to Christianity, or, more disastrously, embrace a total cynicism.

Another version of this disillusionment is felt by those who collapse into resentment on unmasking their chosen guides as nothing more than deceivers. In the modern Buddhist world, it is sometimes hard for neophytes to distinguish the authentic masters from the snake-oil salesmen. They have similar names, they sometimes come from the same places, and, nowadays, they've even got the titles. The one difference, which should be obvious (but unhappily may not be to us, owing to our inexperience in such matters, and the general newness of Buddhism in the West), is that the purveyors of snake-oil long ago cast off the shackles of fidelity to true Buddhism in word or deed. Maybe that's why we like them to begin with – they're flexible. Perhaps, in some way, they remind us of ourselves.

In many cases, we have embraced a spurious system that is Buddhist in name only, and, what is more, we have often embraced masters who are masters in name only. No wonder we are disappointed when we discover that Buddhism is far from what we imagined. How the truth is going to hurt when we find out how we have allowed ourselves to be deceived.

However, resentment at the phony package we have been sold, or at the flourishing of the fakes, is somewhat misplaced. First of all, we gave them their power, out of a mixture of credulity and lack of curiosity about Buddhism itself. Secondly, our motivation, all too often, was essentially frivolous and led us to prefer the fashionable and famous over the authentic but unglamorous. In any event, the truth is that fakes have always ridden on the heels of the authentic, whether it's Devadatta[30] stalking the Buddha, or the numerous examples of fakes and fakery in Tibet called out by masters as far apart as Sakya Pandita in the thirteenth century or Patrul Rinpoche in the nineteenth century.

As Sakya Pandita says:

A master too should be perceived as a master
If he is in accord with the sutras and tantras.
However, master or not, be indifferent towards him
If he does not teach in accord with the Buddha's
  teaching.[31]

At the time when Sakya Pandita was pouring the cold water of clarity on fakery, there were enough people serious about Buddhism itself, and not the transient charisma of certain masters of fake Buddhism, to heed his advice, and this ensured the continuation of the teaching. In this way, disillusionment with the inauthentic was not poisoned by resentment, precisely because of a wish for engagement with the real teachings. Today, I'm not sure there are enough people who want Buddhism undiluted.

Saints and sinners exist side by side now as they always have in Buddhism. Our focus should be to learn the teaching from those masters who, in their actions and instructions, embody the old qualities of Buddhism. In this manner, we will learn to discriminate wisely, as grown-up people do, so that we don't get tricked by the salesmen offering us their poisonous remedies. However, we will only want to do this if our motivation is well-grounded.

Unfortunately, we've not understood that this is the way it's always been, and – until all sentient beings have attained enlightenment – the way it's always going to be. So, sometimes, we begin with naïve and over-exaggerated 'devotion' to a teacher who, we imagine, floats somewhere above the tiresomeness of interpersonal responsibilities (except to us, of course, because we don't really mind how anyone except us is treated). It's this credulity and ignorance concerning the actual role of teachers that gets some into the beds of some unscrupulous 'masters', and others into the proxy armies that the empire-building teachers form out of their naïve followers to fight their battles and disable their opponents for them. Incidentally, happily for these masters, there's no one quite so fanatical as their impressionable followers in policing the territory of dispute with the weapons of anathemas, exclusions and bans that are a feature of the contemporary politics of Buddhism. Of course, it is all so much easier than practising the dharma, with its constant challenge to the comfort of our self-clinging mind.

Inevitably, in the end, the bottom will fall out. For some, this happens once they recognise that genuine Buddhism is utterly different than they had imagined and they recoil in disgust from how different from our contemporary opinions it really is. Others will discover that the fakery that they have swallowed cannot provide support and guidance in a time of difficulties. For yet others, there will be the devastating understanding that they have allowed themselves to be manipulated, and, in the moment of disillusionment, where once there was a fanatical devotion, there will spring up an equally fanatical resentment. It will be all the sharper for the wound to their self-love and vanity. Previously god-like masters – variously father, mother, lover and best, best friend – will now be condemned as vampire chiefs leading a conspiracy of manipulative demons. One can only feel a great sorrow for those caught in such a situation, whether it is through their own credulity or simply youth and innocence.

However, it's time to grow up. It requires that we shed our illusions – in short, become properly disillusioned – because there is no other way to avoid the extremes of credulity and resentment. We have created a 'Buddhist' samsara for ourselves, perhaps with the help of people whom we should have looked at a little more carefully. After all, as Patrul Rinpoche says, to follow a fake master ends up with us jumping off the cliff with the one in whom we have placed our trust, hand in hand, to mutual destruction.

Therefore, to avoid the misfortune of making faulty connections with Buddhism, there is a pressing need for would-be practitioners to be instructed in how to cultivate the appropriate motivation for the study and practice of the dharma. Only this will give them a steadiness of purpose and clear-sightedness about the genuine aims of spiritual practice. That such cultivation is necessary is a point made succinctly in the cycle of teachings known as 'Parting from the Four Attachments' taught by the Sakya master Kunga Nyingpo back in the twelfth century. As it says there:

If you have attachment to this life,

You are not a practitioner of the Buddha's teaching.
If you have attachment to the realm of cyclic existence,
You don't have renunciation.[32]

Such questioning of our motivation must not be evaded if we are to benefit from our involvement with the Buddha's teaching, for we can buy the right books (containing the Buddha's teachings), attend the right centres (where people are practising sincerely), and even make retreats (that seem to be in accord with the traditional teachings), and yet still not be practising it.

As the Buddha said:

Everything rests on the point of intention.[33]

What prevents a 'performance' of Buddhism being the real thing is when our motivation for practice is contaminated by the so-called 'eight worldly concerns', the ephemeral goals that render impossible any glimpse of the transcendental freedom that is the proper goal of Buddhist practice. In this sense, the 'eight worldly dharmas', as they are also known, are the very opposite of Buddha's dharma. They comprise four pairs of motivating factors: determination to acquire pleasure and not pain, gain and not loss, fame and not notoriety, praise and not blame.

In everyday life, they push our continuously discontented mind forward. It should be no surprise, then, that when we first encounter Buddhism, the eight worldly concerns simply shift their focus from gross objects, such as acquisition of property, to the more subtle worldly rewards to be gained through Buddhism, such as the acquisition of the 'property' of status as a spiritual practitioner.

It is for this reason that another great Sakya master, Drakpa Gyaltsen, declared:

When one is attached to this life,
Even one's ethical discipline is contaminated by the eight
  worldly concerns.[34]

He also said:

The meditator who is focussed on this life
Is still busy even when he is in meditative seclusion.[35]

In other words, for such a person, worldly concerns still dominate times of retreat – that is, periods of time during which one temporarily leaves one's worldly life and enters into meditative seclusion, dedicated exclusively to spiritual practice in accordance with specific retreat instructions of one's master. In this respect, to understand the Buddha's teachings as merely a method for improving our status and situation within the cycle of suffering falls far short of the freedom to which they summon us.

The remedy to the eight worldly concerns taught in 'Parting from the Four Attachments' is to contemplate the four themes comprising (i) the preciousness of our human life, (ii) impermanence and death, (iii) action (cause and result, which, as we discussed earlier, in Chapter 3, we refer to as 'karma') and (iv) the defects of cyclic existence. Without the transformation in our values brought about by these four contemplations, engagement in spiritual practice will only serve to strengthen our self-centredness. Thus the remedy for the subversion of our practice to worldly ends is to develop a profound and thoroughgoing disillusionment with our everyday world of illusions.

The first contemplation exhorts us not to squander the precious opportunity that we have found. Right now, poised as we are between birth and death, we possess the freedom and capacity to reflect, which is characteristic of human life, and also the good fortune to have met with Buddhism. We thus possess an indispensable working basis, by which our potential to become a Buddha can be fulfilled: a potential which is inherent in the very nature of our mind, but which we, as humans who have met with the Buddhist path, have a unique opportunity to realise.

Yet the inspiration generated by attentiveness to this precious moment of our human existence must be tempered and simultaneously strengthened by acknowledging the fact of impermanence, the second contemplation. This is not the casual acceptance of the impermanence of externalities so familiar to us in our consumption-driven society where everything is disposable, but a heartfelt acknowledgement that there is no conditioned thing, including our own present existence, that escapes death. To know this through deep contemplation is to awaken to the possibilities inherent in this very life, in this very moment, and not to get lost in the pursuit of the ephemera of the eight worldly concerns.

At this point, although we may have engaged to some extent with Buddhist teaching, we may still be mistaking it as a means to some temporary improvement, whether in terms of developing a more refined state of consciousness or gaining a higher type of rebirth within cyclic existence. To overcome such a dilution of Buddhism and its purpose, we need to analyse, in our contemplation, all possible states of life into which we may be born. From top (the realm of the gods) to bottom (the hell realms) and everywhere in between, the cycle of repeated birth and death is suffering. What brings about its various forms of suffering are our choices and consequent actions. The final two contemplations that turn the mind to the teaching of the Buddha thus focus on the suffering which characterises all our experience (the fourth contemplation) and the causes of such experience – that is to say, our actions (the third contemplation).

As long as the intentions underlying our dharma practice remain naïve and unserious, we will only be settling for more suffering. By contrast, through attention to these four themes of contemplation (often called 'the four thoughts') we come to understand that to practise Buddhism with a mind that is not imbued with the values of the Buddha is to sell it short and to settle for less than freedom. Furthermore, a person who has taken these four contemplations to heart – and achieved the thoughtful disillusionment that ensues from this – is not likely to fall prey to the snares and deceits of fake teaching presented by fake masters. Such a person simply will not be impressed by them nor have time for their trickery.

The profoundly disillusioning effect of these contemplations brings to us a sharp clarity about modern culture and our own capacity for self-deception. Until this point, we have been trying to find security and fulfilment in what the modern world offers, but, actually, it seems like everything in modern culture is broken. Everywhere you look, there's nothing to rely on any more. Between countries there are broken treaties; between people there are broken vows. Politicians break their word and preachers break the golden rule. In matters of love, the holy kiss, which was supposed to last for eternity, is forgotten the morning after, and, in matters of religion, the wise men you trusted only wanted to capture your soul and hold it for ransom.

Actually, it's not really what's broken outside that is the problem – it's what's broken inside. We are broken and we cannot trust ourselves any more to be true to anything or anybody. We have no stability of mind or constancy of purpose. Instead, we are so fickle that we are like a monkey jumping from tree to tree, grabbing first one thing, then another, in a ceaseless search for novelty.

What makes things a thousand times worse is that there's so much to excite the monkey nowadays. Everything's laid on for him. He's distracted from distraction by distraction. Every time things get a little difficult or a little boring, he flips the channel, buys a new suit, a new toy, a new face and a brand-new mind. When the going gets rough, the monkey gets going: out of the door.

The one way to turn this around is to discover the strength that commitment brings, a commitment that arises out of our engagement with the four contemplations. Only a resolve to live for more than the moment and for more than ourselves can deliver us from the prison of self-indulgence and weakness. In Buddhism, such resolve is expressed in the various vows and pledges that provide the foundation for the spiritual path. So when we take the 'individual liberation' vows, whether as lay practitioners or monastics, we shape a commitment to refrain from harm as long as we live. In the case of the bodhisattva vow, one's commitment lasts until one has achieved Buddhahood for the benefit of all beings, and, if we receive the tantric vows through Vajra Vehicle initiations, we are resolved to maintain pure vision throughout every aspect of experience. Without such commitments that stretch beyond the immediate present, whatever meditation we might undertake in any of the Buddhist vehicles will have no sustaining force and we will inevitably be blown off course by internal or external obstacles.

Obviously, such commitments should not be undertaken recklessly, but, once made, we should strive to stay right with them, when the magic seems to fade and difficulties turn up, as they always do. Only those who can trust themselves to be true when this happens are worthy of the trust of others. So, it seems to me that the old heroes were the right ones after all – strong people true to their word, whom you could rely on in any situation – the Pale Rider riding off in to the distance, all duty done, and the man sitting quietly under the tree in Bodh Gaya, dissolving the demon of self.

Of course, when we really do examine our true motives, or even our past actions, with unabashed self-honesty, as the four contemplations require, we might become despondent with what we see. Some time ago, I heard someone say that you could sink so low and become so defiled in this world that even your mother and father would not recognise you, but there would always be the possibility that you could turn around, renew yourself and put yourself back on track. However, in the depths of a winter of despair, it's easy to forget this, as the nights of the disturbing emotions get longer and we head for the darkest day, into a deep midnight when it seems everything is shrunk and shrivelled and that nothing will ever come back to life.

Once we were young and full of the promise of summer. Unfortunately, we took so many shortcuts and made so many wrong turns that we're no longer sure how we arrived here or exactly what it was that we came here to get away from. Sometimes, it's so dark that we don't even know what the word 'hope' means anymore. When we look back, we can see that we meant well, but somehow it never turned out the way we intended. There were so many people we promised to help, but we only ended up helping ourselves. There were so many times we swore we'd be true, but we were true only to our own ambition. Once upon a time, we voted for utopia but only helped to build hell. Once upon a time, we called ourselves wise but we only parroted the opinions of fools. Now, when we've squandered so much time, what's up ahead? The slow train from the future is coming down the line and it's picking up speed. Any day now it will be coming round the bend and it sounds like it's on the final run. The summer of enlightenment is a distant dream, and our cold winter is promising to be hard.

However, it's only when, through the four contemplations, we admit how dark it got, when we admit how low we've sunk and how far we've wandered, that a new start is possible. In other words, rather than the shallow disillusionment of those who give up Buddhism because it did not match their foolish expectations, we need the profound disillusionment that makes real practice of the dharma possible. Until then, we are destined to repeat the same old mistakes and selfishness of the past.

How we learn the authentic Buddhist teaching that leads us away from such error is the topic of the next chapter.

Chapter 7
Learning the Craft

Nowadays people seem to arrive at the Buddha's teaching from many different directions. Among those who are not frivolous, some are pushed towards Buddhism because an overwhelming experience shatters their world and leaves them no other choice. Others arrive more gently, perhaps through disillusionment with the shallowness of contemporary culture, as we have just discussed; encountering Buddhism, they find meaning and purpose.

Others come because they are wounded in some way, whether by love or hatred or just by the bitter dance of loneliness. In Buddhism, they discover a salve for their ills. Then there are those who come looking for answers that they couldn't get from religion, philosophy or politics. For them, Buddha's teaching speaks compellingly of mysteries to be solved and truths to be unveiled.

For Buddhism to fulfil any of these promises, we need to know how to learn it. Making this point may seem unnecessary, but I think that, if we don't know how to learn it, we are unprepared for the actual task of discovering what it offers. All too often, our heads are already full of too much information about nothing; there's no space for anything else. It's not likely that such an arrogant and closed mind can learn anything from the Buddha's dharma, as we saw earlier in our discussion of conceit.

In place of imagining that we already know all there is to know, we must have a readiness to learn. We also need to acknowledge that the process of learning will take a lifetime and that the triad of 'hearing, reflecting and meditating' is central to this process, the significance of which gradual three-fold approach we must consider carefully.

As the fourth-century savant Vasubandhu declared:

On the basis of moral discipline,
Practise hearing, reflecting and meditation.[36]

The use of the term 'hearing' signifies that the teaching has always been directly received from others, our teachers, through whom we join the chain of transmission that stretches back to that garden in Varanasi where the Buddha instructed his first disciples. To disregard the unbroken chain of hearing and forage instead for information on 'Buddhism' in books or the internet – that repository of the debris of civilisation – is probably not going to help much. It should be obvious, but if we adopt such a method of 'consuming' the dharma, we are all too likely to select those fragments that appear sympathetic and unthreatening to our already-entrenched opinions and subtle emotional and cognitive imprints. This is surely one of the principal reasons that there are so many distorted versions of Buddhism on the market right now.

In fact, it is this personal transmission of the teaching from teacher to student that has formed the essential substructure on which the continuation of Buddhism rests. So perhaps it's best to listen to educated masters, who can share the Buddha's teaching with us properly. The master, in this respect, is not only intellectually fluent in the teachings but has made a living experience of them and thus can communicate the actual force of the Buddha's dharma. This is true for all levels of Buddhist practice, but is most marked in the Vajra Vehicle, where, without personally receiving initiation and blessings from masters, who themselves are part of such an unbroken line of transmission of spiritual power, our practice will not bear fruit.

However, as we mentioned in the preceding chapter, we must take care in choosing our teachers, because there have always been those who would attempt to sell us a version of their own fabrication while passing it off as something genuine.

Sakya Pandita characterised such behaviour aptly enough:

> After showing the tail of a deer
> The person without any shame sells donkey meat.[37]

Since those who invent their own Buddhism have only their own opinions upon which to draw, we need to rely on those masters who are anchored in a tradition. They could be masters of the Sakya, Kagyu, Geluk or Nyingma, or, for that matter, Theravada or one of the East Asian traditions. The point is that there is a fundamental sanity in these traditions, born out of the fact that they have been the guiding spiritual force in the lives of men and women in generation after generation. Such a grounding in accumulated experience and tested knowledge contrasts dramatically with the weightless prescriptions of the self-appointed.

In any case, one may well wonder whether there's anything truly innovative or daringly revolutionary about the so-called 'new Buddhism' taught by so many of the new style of teachers. One could easily see it as the marketing of the same old conventional set of secular opinions under the guise of Buddhism by people who either disagree with fundamental aspects of the Buddha's teachings or feel the need to supplement them with withered versions of reheated existentialism, or 'Oprah-fied' psychotherapy peddled by those who are not even half as sharp as Freud or Jung.

Such a gutless Buddhism can do little for us. In fact, rather than our coming to resemble what is set forth in Buddha's teachings, this 'Buddhism' only grows to resemble us. In this respect, isn't it clear by now that many attempts to render Buddhism more accessible have only ended up stealing its power? To make Buddhism easier turns out to be to water it down, and that, inevitably, means that the medicine is diluted. Are we so clever today that we need less teaching and practice?

Instead of adjusting the Buddha's teachings in this fashion, we need to focus on the undiluted teaching and let it speak to us, thus allowing a real connection between our intelligence and the actual unmodified Buddhism to take place. This process is the second stage, that of 'reflecting'.

Through this, the force of the teachings, which are sometimes clear, sometimes obscure, will cause a ferment in our mind, and, out of this, we can gradually distil the wisdom of reflection. This requires discipline and bravery – the bravery to dig deep down to uncover our confusion, which can express itself in questions and doubts about the dharma. Here we cannot progress unless we shun the easy evasion of blind faith – for when did blind faith ever lead to wisdom? Instead, we can arrive at certainty in the truth of Buddhism only through direct experience and inferential reasoning.

At this point, some people, particularly those who are suspicious of religion due to the cultural changes we discussed in Chapter 2, may ask whether this stress on certainty assigns Buddhism to the category of philosophy rather than religion. Actually, the question is misplaced. Since the great divorce between religion and philosophy that occurred in the West in the seventeenth century never happened in Asia, all types of thought, from theism to materialism to non-theistic

Buddhism, are better understood as simply 'views' of the nature of reality.

Resolving hesitations and uncertainties, through intelligent and sustained reflection on the teachings that we have heard, leads us in to meditation, where this reflection is translated into actual experience, the final part of the three-fold path to wisdom.

Here, to 'meditate' is to cultivate a direct experience in accord with the teachings we have heard and examined in the prior two stages. This is now a decisive knowledge, since it is first hand. In the final analysis, the truth revealed in meditation is a 'self-cognising wisdom', through which the mind knows its own nature to be an emptiness beyond all dualities without the intermediaries of concept or language, as we will detail in the next chapter. In short, the ultimate truth that is realised through meditation is not the generic image or mental image of reality accessible through hearing and reflecting but the definitive non-dual realisation to which we give the name 'primordial wisdom'. However, such wisdom could not have arisen without the use of language and analytical thinking in the two preceding stages of 'hearing' and 'reflecting'. It is because of this critical point about the indispensability of the preceding stages that those who eschew the work of hearing and reflection and attempt to rely upon meditation alone will only further entangle themselves in the fabrications of ignorant mind.

As the nineteenth-century Nyingma scholar Mipham Rinpoche explained:

If you do not know the nature of phenomena,
However much you meditate
You are still meditating on ordinary concepts.[38]

As we have already made clear, to embark upon this process of 'hearing, reflection and meditation' we need to rely upon suitably qualified masters. Such a teacher is, in effect, transparent, in that we may see through the person of the teacher to the teachings of the Buddha. Teachers themselves are there to assist us in hearing, reflecting and meditating, just as a skilled master craftsman trains his or her apprentices in the mastery of the craftsman's own craft. Thus, one way to distinguish the authentic master from the confidence trickster – Asian or Western – is that the latter points only to himself or herself and not to the Buddha and his teaching, whereas the authentic master is imbued with the generosity of authentic Buddhist teaching.

On our spiritual journey, the same teacher might function in different ways according to the teachings being given and the level of our understanding. It's important to be clear about these distinctions in the role and function of teachers.

Initially, we might well simply understand and relate to the teacher as someone who has been somewhat further down the road and can give us good advice and instruction in the fundamental teachings such as 'the four thoughts that turn the mind to the teaching' that we discussed earlier. Later on, the same master, or a different one, may tutor us in the philosophical systems of 'The Great Vehicle', such as the tenets of the Middle Way, or even give us initiations from the esoteric system of the Vajra Vehicle. In any case, the appropriate response from our side, as a disciple, is respect and gratitude for what the teacher has shared with us.[39]

As we have mentioned earlier, there can seem to be a great distance between us and the days when the traditions of Buddhism held uncontested sway over the culture of much of Asia and helped it shape cultures that, in some respects at least, reflected Buddhism's civilising influence, before the corrosive effects of internal decay and external interference undermined them. However, although external circumstances may change, the way in which realisation of the nature of mind develops is still essentially the same, since the mind itself knows no time. Thus, even today, there are still great masters left for those who want to engage with Buddhist thought through the three-fold method of hearing, reflecting and meditating.

Chapter 8
Meditation

As we have just seen, for Buddhism, meditation is the decisive means by which access to the true nature of reality is to be gained, but it appears that it might have taken on quite a different significance for many today.

One of the most insistent trends in the world of Spirituality Inc. in recent times has been the cult of meditation. It sits well with the growing 'spiritual but not religious' crowd comprising those who seek to wear the fashionable badge of spirituality without the inconvenient baggage of religion, but its popularity also has important implications for Buddhism. Many welcome the turn to meditation as creating opportunities for our tradition. However, the situation might be more complex. It could be that the rise of meditation actually renders Buddhism's development here problematic – such as by providing impotent, ineffective and mis-sold remedies. One danger is that some people, who erroneously think they are encountering the teaching of the Buddha when in fact they are not, will not just reject these fake remedies, but Buddhism as a whole. A second danger is that some may see meditation (which in the Buddhist tradition is the means of viewing reality) as something to shore up one's self, an objective for which Buddhism is uniquely unsuitable.

One can identify two dominant strands of Buddhist-related meditation that are currently enjoying a high degree of visibility. On the one hand, there is the secularised meditation hatched out of Theravada by Western Insight meditation midwives in the 1970s that reached its apotheosis in the 'McMindfulness' boom. This movement routinely minimises and sometimes even denies any connections with Buddhism. In some circles, it has become a habit to dismiss Buddhism in general.

Occupying a somewhat different cultural and spiritual space, however, is a strain of meditation practice that identifies itself as Buddhist but nevertheless proclaims that the spiritual desiderata of the tradition, up to and including enlightenment itself, can be acquired solely though sitting meditation. It avers that contemporary Buddhists need not concern themselves with study, ethical precepts, ritual practice (other than meditation), or practising meritorious activities (that is, activities which increase one's capacity to connect with the teaching). The proponents of the 'just sitting' tendency often claim the mantle of traditional systems, whether Theravada Insight, Japanese Zen, or Tibetan Great Perfection. All share the same assumption that meditation must be as non-conceptual in content as possible, and that all other forms of activity can be largely, if not entirely, discounted.

This contradicts authoritative presentations of Buddhist teaching from all periods of history, which make it clear that there is no sanction for such a stand-alone view of meditation. Indeed, the most clearly-defined and often-cited status of meditation, within Buddhist doctrine and practice, positions it as one of the three trainings, the other two being ethics and wisdom. As Nagarjuna declared in his *Letter to a Friend*:

> In superior moral discipline, superior wisdom
> And superior contemplation, one must constantly train.
> More than one-hundred-and-fifty trainings
> Are truly included in these three.[40]

Without the ethical development brought about by training in ethics, which Nagarjuna refers to as 'the foundation of all qualities',[41] meditation will be spiritually fruitless.

When one examines, in particular, the place of meditation in the Vajra Vehicle (the esoteric teachings derived from the tantras, which we will discuss briefly in Chapter 9), one finds again that meditation is not considered a self-sufficient means of spiritual accomplishment. Within that tradition, it comes second in the triad of view, meditation and action. *View* signifies the correct vision of reality that the master imparts to the student, and *meditation* signifies the subsequent development and stabilisation of the glimpse afforded by this introduction. Thus, it is only through both view and meditation, together with their enactment and testing in *action*, that one could even approach spiritual accomplishment.

As expressed by the Kagyu hierarch Karmapa Rangjung Dorje:

> Certainty in this view arises from severing doubts about the basis.
> The essential point of meditation is to maintain this without distraction.
> The supreme activity is mastery of this meditation.[42]

Concerning the related demand for an entirely non-conceptual form of meditation, the clamour to re-imagine bare sitting as the core or entirety of the practice animates a considerable part of the refashioning of Buddhism. While mere sitting may produce certain mental effects, one must nonetheless ask: *to what end?* Unallied with any ethical imperative and directed by unexamined assumptions, meditation becomes a purely internal mental technology. In other words, such allegedly non-conceptual meditation will, at best, be a neutral activity. Unmoored from the Buddha's teachings, it does not lead to the particular compassion and wisdom that he taught.

As Mipham Rinpoche explains:

Most settling meditations without analysis
Can produce a mere calm-abiding,
But, from this, certainty will not arise.
If certainty,
The one eye of the path of liberation,
Is abandoned,
The obscurations cannot be dispelled.[43]

Thus authentic meditation necessarily involves two stages – calm-abiding and insight. Some modern proponents of insight argue that one can dispense with calm-abiding. Unfortunately, however, attempting to practise insight on its own, without a degree of stillness brought about by calm-abiding, only leads to further entanglement in conceptual knots.

As Shantideva said:

Knowing that the disturbing emotions
Are overcome by insight
Endowed with calm-abiding,
I shall first practise calm-abiding.[44]

Calm-abiding is a settled one-pointedness of mind, not a sleepy or blank state. One rests in the experience of the present moment, neither distracted by thoughts of past or future nor anxiously grasping at whatever is arising right now. It is a state that is stable, open and clear, in which thoughts are neither suppressed nor cultivated.

Only once such stillness has become characteristic of one's meditation can one begin to work with the instructions for insight. At first, one should investigate the nature of the objects that seemingly appear to our mind, whether they be visual or any other kind of object. The more we interrogate these objects, the more we will understand that they actually arise in dependence upon our mind, and are, in fact, not separate entities somehow standing out there. The gulf that one has imagined to exist between objects and one's perceiving consciousness is imaginary.

Likewise, when one turns to one's mind itself – the seeming subject who perceives – one cannot find any solidity to it either. Just as apparently existent external phenomena are not to be found, so mind itself cannot be found. Instead, the notions of an 'inside' and an 'outside', a 'subject' and an 'object', 'matter' and 'mind', 'self' and 'other', are just conceptual interpretations that we habitually layer upon the stream of conscious experience. Thus all phenomena are, in fact, nothing other than mind.

Even this stream of experience cannot be established as possessing any substantiality. We cannot discover any of the attributes (such as shape, colour, location or duration) that would mark its existence as a real graspable entity. Yet this lack of any trace of substantiality (of what one would ordinarily conceive of as being 'real') does not consign mind to the status of a mere non-entity, since it is the source of all appearances.

In such a way, all dualistic conceptualisation , the very ground of ignorance about reality, is exhausted in this realisation that the true nature of mind transcends all concepts and designations, including, most importantly, those which assign to it any status as an entity or non-entity – a realisation which is the experiential confirmation of Nagarjuna's Middle Way view.

It is ignorance of these vital points of calm-abiding and insight that frequently leads neophytes to overrate their meditation experiences, occasionally with catastrophic outcomes. Experiences of non-conceptuality, bliss, or clarity, all of which are common but fleeting, leave some individuals imagining they are enlightened. However, contrary to their excited imaginings, the stages of ethical and contemplative refinement that culminate in authentic enlightenment are extraordinarily subtle and far-reaching, making such a definitive achievement comparatively rare (despite being potentially achievable by all, and not gainsaying the fact that there are numerous practitioners who exhibit some of the qualities obtained by serious practice of the Buddhist path).

The more fortunate among those enthusiasts subsequently discover that they have fooled themselves. The less fortunate, though perhaps more ambitious, simply proceed to redefine the actual nature of enlightenment so as to preserve their status. 'Enlightenment' becomes merely a term for a transient meditation experience. This gets around the awkwardness of the fact that such 'enlightened' meditators are still, after all, beings subject to disturbing emotions and ignorance. In fact, the actual profound, radical and irreversible nature of complete enlightenment is, whilst achievable, far beyond such limited and narrow conceptions. The very occurrence of these unfortunate attempts to redefine the meaning of 'enlightenment' highlights the importance of developing a correct understanding of the meaning of enlightenment (as distinct from our pre-existing prejudices) as part of the path.

More seriously, such free-floating meditation, disconnected from its proper place in the Buddhist path, is ripe for subversion to whatever political or economic ends its proponents prefer. It easily absorbs the values of the most unsavoury elements of our culture, whether it be the ruthlessness toward the life of the unwanted young or old that dresses itself up as 'liberation', or the patrician unconcern with those left behind today by post-industrialisation. In other words, many meditators, thinking that they are practising the essence of Buddhism, remain completely ignorant of the ideological values that might come to underpin decontextualised meditation. In our society, such values are those embodied in a ruthless individualism congenial to both the market and the state.

To compensate for this, such a style of meditation in the West often grounds itself in a mélange of self-indulgence and gesture politics masquerading as compassion – a 'compassion', it must be said, that cannot see beyond self-regard. The result is the same vapid posturing that dominates so much of contemporary culture.

If current trends continue, meditation will become a mere app for stress-free living. It will simply come to accommodate the harmful consumption-driven lifestyles that still characterise much of life in wealthy countries. In such a scenario, meditation would serve as a reinforcing agent to stabilise delusion, rather than a force that liberates us from delusion and self-centredness.

In any event, it seems foolish to deny that the severing of meditation from ethics and wisdom could have unfortunate consequences. Given that many of us have little Buddhist education, the potential for the misappropriation and derailing of Buddhism is huge.

One of the major problems for the continued transmission of Buddhism is the failure of people to recognise the importance of training in Buddhist ethics, particularly the four key precepts of refraining from taking life, theft, sexual misconduct and untruthfulness. For the Buddhist path to be at all effective, training in Buddhist ethics is indispensable. Many people, regrettably, know so little about Buddhism that they do not have a world-view that supports such training.

One possible solution for this dilemma is to teach meditation alone initially, in order to meet what seems to be a popular demand, and then later on introduce the ethical and philosophical dimensions of the dharma. However, unless links are made quickly and authoritatively to the other two trainings – ethics and wisdom – a negative outcome is more likely to develop from this strategy than genuine spiritual progress. There might be some minor meditative experiences that develop, but these will all too easily lead to an emboldening of the 'self'.

Perhaps the best answer for our dilemma is to teach all three trainings more or less simultaneously, while being mindful that there exists a logic to their sequential development. A student's progress in one training will enable progress in the others. As the re-ordering of one's life, brought about by moral training, creates the environment for meditation, the stillness of mind created by meditation will make possible the examination of reality that is the hallmark of wisdom. In the next chapter, we will discuss how such wisdom is to be allied with compassion.

Chapter 9
Wise Compassion

From London to Los Angeles, it seems like it's the age of compassion. I hear it everywhere I go. Politicians are selling it, advertisers are packaging it, gurus are preaching it, and movie stars are wearing it. Maybe we Buddhists should be happy about this fashion for compassion. After all, as the bodhisattva Avalokiteshvara says:

> Whoever wishes to attain the state of a Buddha does not need to train in many teachings but needs only to train in one – that of great compassion.[45]

I wonder, though, if we are not deceiving ourselves and that, in truth, it's simply the age of sentimentality. Perhaps genuine compassion, the wish that beings be free from suffering and the causes of suffering, has been confused with sentimentality, its ugly step-sister. Whereas compassion looks outwards to others, sentimentality is just concerned with ourselves and our feelings – a seductive force in a culture where we want to feel good about ourselves all the time. Consequently, sentimentality has little regard for the actual well-being of those for whom it pretends to feel concern. It's like the foolish parent, who, to feel good about herself, indulges every whim of her child with predictably disastrous results.

Sentimentality craves applause – an applause that comes at no personal cost nowadays, if you support whatever is the currently approved cause, organisation or party. Indeed, voting 'compassionate' gets you a free pass on your own personal behaviour, in addition to invitations to all the best parties, where the great humanitarians and philanthropists network.

Unfortunately, few of us in Western Buddhist circles are free of this confusion between sentimentality and compassion. This is to be regretted intensely, since it's vital that our understanding of compassion should be consistent with Buddha's tough and clear-minded teachings. As he insisted, unless people live an ethical life (that is, incidentally, 'ethical' according to the ethical precepts that the Buddha explained in his teachings on moral behaviour, as opposed to 'ethical' in the sense used nowadays as appertaining to the often materialistic and self-serving precepts laid down by modern self-appointed 'ethicists'), the happiness that one might wish for them will be unobtainable. So, wise judgement and compassion must be married – and not opposed, as, in our sentimental culture, they all too often are.

Here we should examine the precise nature of compassion. A particularly serious focus of such an examination should be its relationship to wisdom, since it is imperative that our compassion is always a 'wise compassion'. Otherwise it will achieve little that is truly beneficial.

As the highly accomplished master Saraha said:

> Whoever meditates on emptiness without compassion
> Will not walk on the supreme path,
> And whoever meditates exclusively on compassion
> Will not be liberated from the cycle of suffering,
> But whoever unites them will attain the non-dwelling
> nirvana.[46]

As we discussed in Chapter 2, wisdom, at its most profound, severs our erroneous assumption that we possess a permanent, singular and autonomous identity – in short, a 'self'. It is this assumption that has fractured our world, since fixation upon 'self' necessarily and inevitably brings in its wake the notion of 'other'. Part conceptual and part emotional, this fracture underlies our habitually selfish motivation and actions, the very factors implicated in all suffering, and renders compassion impossible. However, to awaken from the bewitchment cast by the illusion of self is always possible, since, in the final analysis, it is a mistaken way of reading the world and our experience.

Compassion, in its turn, dissolves the fiction of self through its concern for others. Understood in this way, compassion is not a mere arbitrary sentiment but a response to others that is grounded in the ultimate truth of emptiness, that self and other are mutually dependent and hence empty of inherent existence. To put it another way: at the most profound level, compassion and wisdom are two faces of one reality. We term this 'bodhichitta' the 'thought of enlightenment' – a force that is both the impetus that causes us to embark upon the path of the Great Vehicle, and, ultimately, is the awakened mind of a Buddha.

Both wisdom and compassion are thus 'natural' in the sense that they are rooted in the actual nature of reality, the recognition of which dissolves the delusion of an inherently existent 'self' and 'other'. One might say, therefore, that to act selfishly is an expression of a mistaken view of the world and, correspondingly, to respond to another's experience of suffering is already, to some extent, to relax the grip of such erroneous views and one's consequent imprisonment in self-interest. In other words, when alertness to others sparks compassion, the narrow walls of one's habitual selfishness are undermined. At the same time, this more open-hearted manner of relating to the world facilitates the growth of wisdom, the principal focus of which is precisely the absence of the abiding self, to which one has clung in error. Incidentally, we might be afraid of even attempting to develop such open-heartedness or to dissolve our own self-interest, fearing the consequences of doing so; however, in fact there is a great strength in an attitude that genuinely privileges the needs of others over oneself, since because it is self-clinging that is the root of our suffering, the consequences of privileging others can only, paradoxically, be happiness.

This understanding of compassion gives it a 'naturalness' that distinguishes it, for example, from the account of compassion in the Christian tradition, where it issues from the belief that man owes love to his neighbour because that neighbour is created by God in his own image. Here in Buddhism, the flow of compassion does not originate from some superior being, but as a natural consequence of the fact that it is mistaken to privilege our own need for happiness over that of our neighbour, since the delusion of selfhood that impels us to do so is just that: a delusion.

Of course, one must concede that, in comparison to the Jewish and Christian arguments for compassion, which possess a certain poetic beauty, the post-religious have few grounds for any appeal to compassion (if they take their own beliefs seriously), since beings, for them, are merely machines; though such people may well, on occasion, indeed act with compassion, we might consider that it is often the result of a residual (if unacknowledged) religious inheritance.

Incidentally, while we are discussing the 'naturalness' of compassion, we must also distinguish this Buddhist understanding of reality and its relationship to compassion from commonly expressed 'New Age' notions about reality, such as 'all is one' or 'we are all one'. Such views are not only philosophically incoherent, as Shantarakshita[47] and other masters have pointed out, but, because they deny change and denigrate the truths of cyclic existence and suffering, they actually render the development of compassion impossible.

The most powerful method of developing such a 'wise heart' is to train in the specific contemplative exercises known as the 'four limitless meditations': loving-kindness, compassion, joy and equanimity. We might train in these in a formal way, as a kind of prayer of aspiration to shape our attitude, by reciting the four meditations (shown in italics below) individually or all together, or more informally but nevertheless in accord with the traditional instructions. Out of these radically altruistic emotions arises bodhichitta, the desire for enlightenment, and, once this has occurred, the 'four limitlesses' then serve as a means of its strengthening and increasing. The term 'limitless' here signifies that, unlike ordinary self-centred feelings of affection, these virtuous social emotions are unlimited in extent, as they encompass all beings without exception and are unlimited in duration, since they will not decline over time.

According to Patrul Rinpoche, there is a considerable advantage in actually beginning the sequence of training in the 'four limitlesses' with equanimity (and not love, as would be indicated in the usual order in which they are set out). He argued that unless we are endowed with the spacious attitude that arises from cultivating such impartiality, the limitlessness of love and so forth will be more difficult to attain.

Equanimity

'May all beings dwell in equanimity without attachment to near ones and aversion to distant ones.'

From the very beginning, it is imperative that we do not mistake equanimity for a callous indifference. Rather it should be understood as an acceptance which allows the transformation of the poison of partisan emotions and bias into an affection for others that has no boundaries. In short, it is the indispensable means that enables us to go on to develop love and compassion to all, including our 'enemies' and others who would do us harm.

The habitual notion of 'friends' and 'enemies' originates from the fundamental misreading of the world that is embodied in our tenacious habits of self-clinging and consequent self-cherishing. Thus, equanimity, by dissolving the seeming solidity of our notions of 'friend' and 'enemy', works backwards to loosen self-clinging itself. In other words, it is an attitude of inclusivity that makes it possible for us to respond to others in a less self-interested and self-defensive way.

It might be useful at this point to consider whether the reason that one is currently attached to some beings as 'near' and others as 'distant' is that one has simply forgotten the constantly shifting nature of relationships. Indeed, it would be appropriate to wonder: 'Who actually is my "friend" and who is my "enemy"?' and, 'What makes someone a friend and another an enemy?'

In this respect, Nagarjuna says:

> Fathers become sons; mothers become wives (in the cycle of rebirth).
> Enemies become friends, and vice versa (in the cycle of rebirth).
> Since that is so,
> There is no certainty in the cycle of birth and death.[48]

Additionally, even our very parents or children could be enemies or creditors from former lives. So, since relationships are unstable in this way, it is surely right to develop a flexibility of mind rather than grasping at temporary appearances as being utterly fixed. If we look even within this life, we can see the fluidity with which relationships change; we can then consider how much more so this might happen over a sequence of lives.

In fact, it's not all that certain whether those who seem to benefit us now are really doing so and whether those who appear to harm us are, in actuality, really detrimental to our well-being. To take just one example, there are seemingly loving parents who damage a child when, fearing to demand anything of their child, they do not help it to develop moral discipline. Equally, there are other parents who are so ambitious for worldly success for their child that they do their utmost to discourage them from pursuing spiritual development, as was famously the case with King Shuddhodhana, father of the Buddha.

On the other hand, those who seem to be difficult to us may actually be our benefactors. At the very least, they definitely provide us with the opportunity to train in patience, a virtue which occupies such a key position on the spiritual path. As Geshe Langri Thangpa points out in his *Eight Verses of Mind Training*:

> When someone whom I have benefited,
> And in whom I have placed great hope,
> Acts with extremely inappropriate harm,
> May I see him as my true spiritual friend.[49]

In the actual sessions of meditation on equanimity there are three stages of training as follows.

First, commence by settling the mind in a relaxed state free from its habitual categorising of whatever arises into 'good' or 'bad', 'pleasant' or 'unpleasant'. When thoughts of particular people or groups come up, do not rush to label or classify them. Instead, without aversion to some and attachment to others, simply consider things in a neutral manner – neither harmful nor beneficial, but just as phenomena that arise and pass away.

Secondly, develop the outlook that, among all these beings, absolutely everyone has been a parent to you.

As Nagarjuna says:

If one could count one's mothers with beads the size of
  juniper seeds,
They would cover more space than the entire earth.[50]

Unfortunately, with the incessant turning of the wheel of
birth and death, we have forgotten each other, and, most
importantly, we have forgotten the previous acts of kindness
that others have shown us.

Finally, train in these contemplative exercises until you
feel the same acceptance and affection towards all beings as
for your own present parents.

In everyday life, you can continue the training by letting
go of the reflex that instantly categorises and reacts to
whatever is encountered. To pause and simply be attentive
to the textures of each situation as it manifests will help
you establish the balance and gentle strength that are the
hallmarks of equanimity. It is not that we are seeking to shut
down or deny the reflex but rather to let go as soon as it arises,
instead of clinging to it (as is our usual tendency).

To convey the quality of equanimity, Patrul Rinpoche
used the example of a host who prepares a great banquet
to which he or she then invites the entire world. Such an
analogy reminds us again that the measurement of authentic
equanimity is an affectionate inclusivity and not an apathy or
indifference.

Equanimity is thus a very liberating force once it has
developed, but it would be foolish to underestimate the
strength of our habit of partisanship. Thus, while such bias
can obviously be founded on matters of family, tribe, class,
nation or religion, we should concede that it is just as easy to
base our partisanship on such matters as culture and ideology,
where bias can be disguised as non-emotional and rational.
In short, we may well be as biased as ever now, but nowadays
we merely indulge our partisanship in a more sophisticated
way of marking 'our group' from 'their group'.

Perhaps this underlies the vigilance by which people and language are scrutinised for obedience to the contemporary 'correct' ideologies. By such means, we can more easily identify our side, and, inevitably, exclude the other. Sometimes even notions of compassion are invoked in this categorisation of what is to be judged 'correct' and 'incorrect', and this can mislead us into assuming that fashionable iterations of 'compassion' are identical with the Buddhist sense of this term.

If that indicates the residual strength of partisanship, at the same time we must also be alert to distorted versions of equanimity. One particular such distortion is the belief that people are utterly the same, with any differences between them being either illusory or superficial. Actually, a wise perspective sees that, while it's true that beings are all alike in possessing mind and disturbing emotions and in wishing to possess happiness and to avoid suffering, their opinions, behaviours and cultures are not necessarily identical. In fact, there are often critical differences in such matters, as mere attentiveness to the world will reveal.

This counterfeit equanimity pretends to non-partisanship but it lacks the spaciousness of mind that is a mark of the latter. Neither is it authentically inclusive, for that can only arise when we do acknowledge difference but then go on to extend our capacity for tolerance for those who are distinct from us in manners and opinions. Contrary to this, in believing that everybody is identical, one does not discover equanimity but merely an excuse to remain small-minded. Indeed, it might be suitable to characterise this counterfeit equanimity as akin to a self-absorbed narcissism, since it has no interest or even respect for others. It doesn't really bother to acknowledge them at all. Genuine equanimity (and the rest of the 'limitless meditations') challenge us, by contrast, and that's why they change us for the better.

Yet another distortion of equanimity is evident in the attitude that elects to prefer 'the distant' to the 'near', when, in authentic equanimity, they are regarded equally. Such a deviation in equanimity often results not from any real regard for the 'distant' itself but from a desire to establish a moral superiority to ordinary people with their despised small and vulgar attachments to home, family and so on. One might suggest that this attitude of superiority is merely a form of ego-display and one which actually leads not to equanimity but only to disrespect, contempt and abuse of those who are near and familiar.

Loving-kindness

'May all beings have happiness and the causes of happiness.'

To meditate on loving-kindness is to discover the antidote to the poison of hatred.

As Gyalse Thokme Zangpo, writing in the fourteenth century, declares:

> If I try to defeat external enemies, more will arise,
> So I should turn inwards,
> And, with the armies of loving-kindness,
> Conquer hatred.[51]

As we have discussed above, loving-kindness, like the other three limitless meditations, is unrestricted in object and duration. It's not an ephemeral feeling that will vanish with changing circumstance. As Shakespeare put it:

> love is not love
> Which alters when it alteration finds.[52]

To generate loving-kindness is to be imbued with the wish that others should enjoy happiness in body and mind both at the present time and in the future. Hence the second part of this benevolent wish is the resolve that 'all may have the causes of happiness'. In making such a wish, one is compelled to wish that they come to behave virtuously, since it is only virtue that leads to authentic happiness, and not, as the world imagines, selfish actions of hatred and desire. Selfish actions merely oppose us to reality and condemn us to disappointment and misery. As with equanimity, then, this aspect of loving-kindness demands a measure of wisdom – in this case, it requires sufficient wisdom to see the manner in which a virtuous life is the primary cause of happiness, in accord with how actions ripen in the appropriate results.

The nature of such moral action is defined by Nagarjuna as follows:

> Actions produced by desire, hatred and ignorance are non-virtues.
> Actions produced out of freedom from desire, hatred and ignorance are virtues.[53]

Such considerations force us to acknowledge those occasions when, if we want to cultivate authentic benevolence, we must wish for others things which, due to their own temporarily unclear thinking, they would not wish for themselves. For example, a thief might believe that his future happiness can be assured by his continuing to steal, whereas this belief is actually contrary to the truth, which is that, inevitably, suffering is the eventual consequence of non-virtue. Thus there is a similarity between this aspect of benevolence and the situation of giving, where we are enjoined not to make 'poisonous gifts' which will result in damage to the recipient. Again, one must not consider that developing love to all beings entails a helpless passivity in response to harm done to others or oneself. Such an attitude would only damage the harm-doer, by colluding with the harm-doer's negative intentions and actions. In short, just as, on occasion, to protect a child from the dangerous consequences of its own folly, one is required to demonstrate care in a stern manner, so, as is made clear in the Great Vehicle, authentic love must sometimes be expressed in a firm way that deters harm.

This all means, of course, that what we consider to be happiness and its causes does not inevitably coincide with current worldly opinions. Specifically, in wishing others to have happiness, we are wishing for them to flourish morally, not to abandon themselves to the delusory pleasures of hedonism or a life based upon the abuse of others. Thus, just as with the term 'compassion', we must consider deeply what we mean by 'happiness': it is not those temporary, self-indulgent pleasures that we wish all beings to have, but rather the causes of genuine happiness as a result of their practice of virtuous behaviour.

To meditate upon loving-kindness, consider your present mother and recall all her kindness, and, in doing so, acknowledge your tremendous indebtedness to this person who placed your welfare above her own. As your heart opens with this acknowledgement, you cannot help but make the wish that she 'be endowed with happiness and its causes'. Then resolve to do everything in your power to bring about this happy outcome and make the aspiration that such a state be accomplished.

This vivid sense of indebtedness to your mother reveals the dependent nature of the world. In fact, this indebtedness and connectedness do not just extend to your present mother. In actuality, since the cycle of birth and death is without beginning, there has been more than enough time for all beings to have acted in this way as parent to us. At this point, you should now widen the ambit of your contemplation to encompass other relations – father, siblings and so on – and reflect how each of them has also acted as your mother in previous lives.

At this point, you should be able bring neighbours into the focus of your meditation. From there, remembering that they too have been our parents countless times, you will be able to encompass even apparent enemies with this same benevolence. By following such an expansion in one's inclusiveness, your heart is opened ever more widely until, finally, the whole world of beings becomes the object of your meditation.

Patrul Rinpoche characterised the development of genuine loving-kindness as similar to the love of a mother bird who has prepared a soft bed for her beloved chicks. One might say, therefore, that there is a good-heartedness and cheerfulness in our dealings with others. Anger and irritation dissolve as others' happiness becomes the abiding value in one's life.

One point that might be useful to clarify here concerns the introduction by some people of a meditation on love for oneself into loving-kindness meditation. I'm sure that this is not ill-intentioned, but it doesn't seem to be a teaching presented in the sutras or authoritative treatises. In any case, one need not worry about one's own happiness if one practises loving-kindness. One will inevitably be more positive and happy as one focuses love on others and one's anger and aggression lessen.

A major obstacle that might undermine the authentic practice of loving-kindness is a fear that love cannot be boundless, that one must select some and exclude others, as if loving-kindness were a substance of which there can only be a fixed and therefore limited amount. However, a love that is restricted is not the authentic loving-kindness that has no exclusions. After all, as Sakya Pandita has declared in a moment of drollery:

Even vampires love their own children.[54]

Besides which, love is not a possession owned by a 'self'. It's boundless in nature, precisely because it arises in the space that is devoid of the notion of self.

Compassion

'May all beings be free from suffering and the causes of suffering.'

The meditation on compassion is the remedy for indifference and selfishness. The core of the practice, therefore, is to cultivate an awareness of the plight of others. To be compassionate always proceeds from the question in which one asks oneself: 'What would it be to experience what another experiences?'

Incidentally, one might wonder why the meditation on compassion is customarily taught after the meditation on loving-kindness. However, in reality, it is only the degree of open-heartedness to others engendered by love that makes compassion possible. The encounter with the fact of another's suffering requires that we already have a certain capacity for openness that has been gently created by love, whereas it is often the case that, lacking the positivity established by love, the bare encounter with others' suffering leads either to resistance or, even more deleteriously, to an attitude of aggression.

As is said in the *Jewel Ornament of Mahayana Sutras*:

Compassion flows through the canal of loving-kindness.[55]

Similarly, the breadth of mind established through equanimity permits our compassion to encompass all individuals and all groups. Hence it's not a selective compassion that just responds to the most insistent demands, or to individuals and groups that one finds particularly congenial. In short, it is a limitless compassion.

As with loving-kindness and its alertness to the causes of happiness, to meditate on compassion requires that we do the work of investigating the causes of suffering which have led to others' current ills and which we, therefore, wish them to lose in the future. In doing so, one comes to understand that it is always non-virtuous actions, motivated by the disturbing emotions and founded upon the mistaken clinging to the notion of self, which are implicated. The causes of suffering thus arise in the disordered heart.

As that is the case, those who presently behave without virtue must also be the focus of our compassion, just as much as those they afflict, since they are creating the very source of their own future suffering.

The stages of meditation follow those already established for loving-kindness meditation. It begins specifically with what is termed 'compassion towards sentient beings'.

Commence by considering your present mother. Having earlier recalled her kindness and your indebtedness to her, now you should reflect on the myriad forms of suffering she faces. Furthermore, though she wants to be free of suffering, she does not know how this might be achieved. Tragically, many of the attempts she makes to become free of suffering, as with her attempts at happiness, produce only the opposite result. Thus you cannot help but feel the strong wish that she be free from sufferings and the non-virtuous behaviour which generates future suffering. Then strive to convert that wish into a firm resolve and conclude it with the prayer that it might come to be.

At this point, extend this compassionate wish to other relatives and, from there, to other beings, both neighbours and enemies, until, finally, the whole world is included in the range of your compassionate gaze. Here prior familiarity with the four contemplations known as the 'four thoughts', which we discussed earlier, in Chapter 6, and, particularly, that concerning suffering, will lend your contemplation on compassion an especial strength.

Such is the meditation on compassion that takes as its object beings as they appear.

Subsequently, you should meditate on 'compassion to phenomena', signifying that your compassionate attitude includes an acknowledgement of the non-virtuous factors, such as the disturbing emotions, that underpin the suffering that beings experience.

Thirdly, meditate on 'compassion without a referential object'. In this most subtle perspective, our compassion is fused with the understanding that, rather the solid independent entities that they imagine themselves to be, beings are empty of any intrinsic nature, and it is their deluded vision in this respect that is the root of their suffering.

One way to extend this meditation, in one's dealings with the world, is to approach each encounter with others with the unspoken question: 'What can I do for you?' Furthermore, you should be careful not to exclude any single person or sentient being from this. Thus pay equal attention to the highest and the lowest among those you meet.

In general, this process should leave us with a sense of gratitude for others. To feel gratitude is to look beyond ourselves and to step outside the walls of pride. When we ask what we can do for those who have done everything for us, we acknowledge our dependence upon them. From this recognition, a genuine kindness can grow and dissolve the seed of hatred.

To describe the intensity of the attitude developed through meditation on compassion, Patrul Rinpoche compared it to the unbearable emotion of an armless mother witnessing her child drowning.

The authentic development of 'limitless compassion' is one that encompasses all beings in their unique individuality, while sentimentality and other forms of fakery merely parody and subvert it. For instance, preference for the group over the individual (which is just one example of fake teachings on so-called 'compassion') blinds us to the stubborn reality that there cannot be a genuine concern for others unless it is rooted in the intimacy of the particular, because the world is made of a limitless array of particulars. This is the reason why, in the tradition of Buddha, we invariably commence our meditative training in compassion by a focus on the individual – usually, our present mother – and work outwards in continually widening circles of inclusivity until all are brought into our 'family'.

In this respect, one cannot help but recall how it is so often the case that 'apostles' of 'compassion' and 'the general welfare' are people who have little regard for the actual individuals in their life. One sees how it can be that, once these sentimentalists with their compassionate programmes are in power, the way to the tumbrils and the guillotine is clear for anyone who transgresses the mores of this fake 'compassion': 'A Sentimental Education' indeed!

As Blake has it:

He who would do good to another must do it in Minute Particulars. General Good is the plea of the scoundrel, the hypocrite and the flatterer.[56]

Another perversion of compassion is the sentimentality that affects to see humans as intrinsically or naturally good. It blithely believes that, with a little adjustment of the external circumstances, everything will be perfect. Such a notion is entirely contrary to the Buddha's teaching. Lest someone invoke the teaching of the 'buddha nature' here, one should understand that, unlike the sentimental view, the buddha nature is not to be identified with the self or ego. The buddha nature is not, in this sense, one's 'true self' beneath the veneer of artificial civilisation (as the Romantics imagined) but mind itself, which, although naturally luminous and empty, is presently obscured by ignorance and disturbing emotions. Hence, while it possesses the potential to become enlightened, it is, at this moment, the basis of both the bliss of nirvana and the suffering of birth and death.

Right now, beings are dominated by these obscurations of ignorance and the disturbing emotions, and, as a result, inflict and experience suffering. It is this undeniable fact that is the ground of compassion – not an indifference, which would be the result of considering beings to be intrinsically good. Thus, authentic compassion recognises the force of non-virtue. It is sufficiently tough-minded (one might equally say 'sufficiently wise') not to have to deny the way the world is. Unfortunately, by contrast, sentimentality crowds out compassion and tells lies about the world.

In conclusion, we must beware the possibility that, out of an insufficient understanding of compassion in the teachings of the Buddha, one will hurry to ally Buddhism with whatever ideologies intone the term 'compassion' most seductively. Such systems usually promise that a state of general perfection can be attained just by external changes, but, as we have already discussed, such a view is not Buddhist – apart from anything else, it is a denial of karma, the law of cause and effect. The story of the failure of King Mune Tsenpo's well-intentioned but unwise policy of redistribution of wealth in eighth-century Tibet is somewhat instructive in this regard.[57] Thus, if one has the compassionate wish that people's situation might be improved, the best thing one could do would be to inspire people to practise virtue by practising virtue oneself, or, in the case of those qualified to do so, by repeating the teachings of the Buddha in response to specific requests (for Buddhist teachings are only to be given in response to a request). Incidentally, it is not by some form of coercion or compulsion that beings are inspired to practise virtue, since it is likely such actions would be a form of self-clinging for the one compelling, not to mention a source of resentment for those being compelled.

Joy

'May all beings never be separate from the (sacred) state that is without sorrow.'

Therefore, to meditate upon joy is to rejoice in the possession by others of the very happiness and consequent freedom from suffering that we have wished for them. Its specific remedial effect is to dissolve any tendency for jealousy that might corrupt our altruism.

Jealousy and envy are rooted in a 'zero-sum game' notion of happiness, in which another's happiness is experienced by oneself as a reduction of the 'portion' of happiness left to oneself. It is an imbalanced attitude which seeks to control and retain everything desirable for itself and thus, in the final analysis, sees everyone else as a potential competitor.

One might now, of course, fondly imagine that, in comparison to those sunk in 'non-spiritual' ways, a refined and spiritual person such as oneself could never be harbouring such base emotions as jealousy and competitiveness. However, such an assumption merely confirms the requirement to be unsparingly honest with oneself in examining one's emotions.

As before, you should practise this meditation in stages, commencing from those presently dear to you, then extending the meditation to those to whom you are currently indifferent, and, finally, culminating in a meditation that encompasses all beings. Earnestly think that, whatever happiness and good fortune they might possess at this time, they may come to have more – so that, for instance, a beautiful person may have more beauty or a rich person may have more wealth. By considering how much their happiness is increased, your own heart rejoices in this. You should continue with such a series of contemplations until any tendency to envy has been dissolved.

Patrul Rinpoche compared the feeling of joy at others' good fortune to the joy felt by a mother camel, a most affectionate mother, when she is reunited with her lost child.

Incidentally, it is important nowadays to be alert to the clever way in which jealousy can disguise itself as a demand for 'fairness', a demand which can then pretend to be disinterested and even compassionate. Actually, whatever we might wish, beings have particular fortunes, whether good or bad, in accord with their choices and actions. Of course, it should hardly need stating that the purpose of these teachings on cause and effect is not so that we may feel arrogant about our own happiness and contemptuous of others; instead, these teachings are to enable us to identify how the world works and how happiness is obtained for oneself and others – that is, by the practice of virtue. Thus we should concentrate on making merit if we wish for future good fortune, and not seek to appropriate someone else's fortune or do so on behalf of another.

As Shamar Konchok Yenlak explains:

If we desire to be happy, we should understand that as a
    sign that we should make merit.[58]

And as Patrul Rinpoche says:

One spark of merit is worth a mountain of effort.[59]

One way of assessing whether a passion for fairness is genuinely altruistic is to examine its driving force. In many cases, unhappily, we will have to conclude that it is resentment and hatred that excite us more than a concern for the unfortunate. This is why linking Buddhism to ideologies of 'fairness' is perilous (even though it has a certain appeal, because of its seeming proximity to compassion) because such ideologies, due to the poison that inspires them (openly or not, and whether or not such ideologies are styled as 'well-intentioned'), usually end up unleashing hatred and violence in the world.

There is a wonderful paradox in the 'four limitless meditations'. They demand and force us to go beyond our habitual selfishness, but, as one practises them, we discover that they constitute a joyful and easy path. They are a path upon which every sentient being becomes our friend who inspires us on the path. It is with this in mind that Shantideva says:

> One should venerate sentient beings and Buddhas
> equally.[60]

Those beings who are currently deprived of happiness provide us with the opportunity to find the capacity for love, and those afflicted by suffering inspire us to compassion, both of which virtuous emotions have the power to transform our present life so radically. Then, even more significantly, these meditations serve as catalysts which bring about the dawning within us of 'bodhichitta', the urge for enlightenment, for the question that love and compassion come to provoke is simple: 'How can I truly place beings in a state of happiness and of freedom from suffering?'

Of course, to ask this question is to be confronted immediately with the sober knowledge that right now, as an ordinary person, embroiled in one's selfish perceptions and habits, one does not possess the ability to accomplish such an aim. Furthermore, in looking around, one can see that the same is true of all beings, whether they be the lowliest or the most exalted, for all are, alike, imprisoned by self-clinging. However, a Buddha, endowed with the three qualities of wisdom, compassion and power, understands the precise causes of the suffering experienced by others and the way to freedom from such oppression; embraces all with unvarying affection, since he or she is free from the slightest trace of selfishness; and is unrestricted in his or her ability to work for others, since he or she is not imprisoned by self-concern.

Thus the four limitless meditations create the spaciousness of heart and mind in which bodhichitta, the resolve to attain the level of a Buddha for the benefit of all beings, arises. It emerges from the universal acceptance of others, that is, equanimity; from the wish to place them in happiness, that is, loving-kindness; from the determination to be able to free all from suffering, which is compassion; and from the joyfulness that rejoices as these wishes begin to be fulfilled.

The wonderful insight present within the Buddha's teachings is most evident here. We understand from the fundamental instructions that self-centredness is the root of our suffering, and therefore one cannot aim for one's own freedom alone but must surrender that form of self-privileging to work for the liberation of others. To do otherwise would be comparable to leaving one's relatives behind to perish in a burning house while fleeing oneself. Thus, in the end, one must generate bodhichitta and in such a manner enter the 'Great Vehicle'.

One might ask at this point if the Buddha's renunciation did not signify a disregard for his loved ones, when, developing renunciation, he physically separated himself from his family to practise in solitude, thereby abandoning them and others close to him, seemingly contrary to this spirit of love. In fact, immediately upon his enlightenment, Buddha shared the dharma with his mother Mayadevi (an event so significant that it is commemorated as one of the four great festivals of the Buddhist tradition), and subsequently with his wife, his son, his father and his beloved aunt Prajapati.

The significant point here, however, is that, without an element of detachment, genuine love is impossible. Even within our families and friendships, effective love requires a measure of detachment. Consider how wise parents are able to set aside their attachment to their own ambitions for their children and think instead of what is actually beneficial for them. Consider also how often self-clinging can insinuate itself in to a natural love for one's family and corrupt in to a narrowness that sets off one family from another or even turns brother against brother. Yet in the contemplative methods of the Buddha's teachings, the love we already feel for our parents or children, far from blocking a wider love, is actually the source that makes it possible.

In other words, although we are aiming at an all-inclusive loving-kindness, unrestricted by partiality that divides the world into 'mine' and 'yours', this needs to start in the simple unfeigned connections we have with those nearest to us right now. Otherwise it will likely be no more than a vague abstraction that 'loves' everybody in general and no one in particular – that is, the kind of 'love' demonstrated by utopians, revolutionaries and others who feel they have a duty to remake the world at large, which usually ends in the gulags and killing fields, as we have discussed earlier.

Our entry to the Great Vehicle is marked by the ceremony of the 'bodhisattva vow', wherein one recites the beautiful words of Shantideva:

> Just like space
> And the other elements such as earth,
> May I always support the life

Of boundless beings,
And until they pass beyond suffering
May I also be the source of life
For all the realms of beings
That reach until the end of space.
Just as the previous sugatas
Gave birth to bodhichitta,
And just as they successively dwelt in the bodhisattva
    practices,
May I give birth to bodhichitta
And accomplish the practices.[61]

For those who make this commitment, the Great Vehicle offers two complementary paths – known as the 'Common' and 'Uncommon' Great Vehicles. The first of these, derived from the discourses of the Buddha, emphasises a gradual approach to enlightenment in which one cultivates the 'six perfections' – giving, ethics, patience, diligence, meditation and wisdom.[62] When practised over a period of many lifetimes, these virtues, the core of which is constituted by compassion and wisdom, eliminate the disturbing emotions and nescience, which, so long as they remain, render enlightenment impossible.

In contrast, the Uncommon Vehicle, or, as it is often known, the Vajra Vehicle, makes enlightenment attainable very swiftly. Although this system, derived from the tantras revealed by the Buddha and other enlightened sources, shares the same ethical impulse and philosophical outlook as the Common Great Vehicle, it places a special emphasis on the continuity of mind that pervades both sentient beings and Buddhas despite their seeming distinction in their respectively unenlightened and enlightened states.

According to the Vajra Vehicle, the nature of mind of both sentient beings and Buddhas is the union of luminosity and emptiness (a tantric restatement of the nature of mind transcending all extremes that was discussed in Chapter 8). As such, both the cycle of suffering and nirvana rest upon this fundamental nature of mind and whether or not it is recognised. Put simply, a Buddha is one who has recognised this, and a sentient being is one who has not. The means for such a liberating recognition is provided by the methods of the Vajra Vehicle, which are primarily the rituals of initiation and subsequent meditation upon the 'deities' who symbolise the primordial pure nature of mind.[63]

Thus, by the methods of the Common or Uncommon Great Vehicle, the journey from unawareness to enlightenment is brought to fulfilment in the wise compassion that is the reality of being a Buddha.

Chapter 10
Beginnings

I'm gazing out the window of the Fairmont Hotel and recalling the past. Every scene went by so fast, but it seems to me that I'm still holding a thread that I picked up as a young boy. It led me here and it will lead me forward. Meanwhile, outside, the waves of the Pacific Ocean are pressing upon the shoreline, and I can see three ships on the horizon. I think of the Buddha's teaching arriving here in the West – this place where wisdom seems to be in exile.

The era of Buddhism's appeal to the West as a fascinating exoticism is drawing to a close, while at the same time it faces major challenges from economic and political developments in Asia. Perhaps most troubling of all, there is a hardening against religion in modern culture. Yet, despite all this, I don't think there's any need to lose our nerve and to try to invent a new Buddhism. It may take some time for it to be properly established, but, fortunately, there continue to be teachers like His Holiness Karmapa and His Holiness Ratna Vajra Rinpoche the 42nd Sakya Trizin, from whom a new generation can learn. Thus I'm confident that the teaching of the Buddha will endure if we practise it with intelligence and fidelity.

In any event, it's really only the first days of the dharma in the West. For us, Buddha is still teaching and Padmasambhava[64] has just been invited to tame the proud. It's time to begin our work for real now.

My mind goes back to that warm summer evening in London long ago. At last, Christmas Humphreys' introductory speech comes to an end and he welcomes the guest of honour. His Holiness the 41st Sakya Trizin begins to speak.

Glossary of Terms

Bodhichitta ('The Thought of Enlightenment')
Bodhichitta may be characterised as the altruistic resolve to achieve the state of a Buddha for the benefit of all beings and the application of this resolve in the spiritual practice that will bring about such a result. There is a second, distinct aspect of bodhichitta, which can be distinguished, namely the transcendental wisdom that recognises the true nature of phenomena, and, as such, is referred to as 'ultimate bodhichitta'.

Bodhisattva
A bodhisattva is someone who has generated bodhichitta and thus has committed himself or herself to achieve the state of a Buddha for the benefit of all beings.

Buddha nature
Buddha nature is the innate potential for enlightenment which exists within all beings but is presently covered by the veils of ignorance and disturbing emotions.

Dharma
In the sense that it is used in this work, 'dharma' signifies the teaching of the Buddha, which is the second of 'The Three Jewels', the others being the Buddha and the Community (sangha) of all those who follow the Buddha and his teaching.

The Great Vehicle ('Mahayana')
'The Great Vehicle' is the path followed by bodhisattvas with the aim of achieving the state of a Buddha and is termed 'great' in contrast to 'The Lesser Vehicle' path where the aim is merely individual liberation and not, as in 'The Great Vehicle', ensuring the liberation of all from suffering.

Karma
'Karma' (literally 'action') signifies the doctrine of action, cause and result, which describes how virtuous, non-virtuous and neutral actions produce results at a later date in the stream of being of the one who commits the action.

Nirvana
Nirvana (literally 'the blowing-out') signifies the extinction of suffering brought about by the practice of the path. In 'The Lesser Vehicle' this is regarded as commensurate with the removal of the disturbing emotions. However, in 'The Great Vehicle' supreme nirvana is characterised as the achievement of the state of a Buddha, who, by removal of the subtle obscuration of ignorance, in addition to that of the disturbing emotions, is endowed with omniscient wisdom and compassion by which he or she can work for the benefit of all beings.

Samsara
The non-Nirvanic state of wandering in the six realms of being (i.e. those of gods, demi-gods, humans, animals, ghosts and the denizens of hell), which states are characterised by suffering and produced through the triad of ignorance, disturbing emotions and actions.

Sugata
The term 'sugata' (literally 'one who has gone to bliss') is an epithet for a Buddha.

Sutra

The term sutra ('discourse') usually refers to one of the three collections in to which the Buddha's general teaching has been aggregated, the others being 'Vinaya' (monastic discipline) and 'Abhidharma' ('philosophy'). When used in contrast to 'tantra' it signifies all three collections.

Tantra

The esoteric scriptural teachings of the Buddhas comprising the tantras which set forth 'The Vajra Vehicle', a special path for obtaining the state of a Buddha. The tantras and the Vajra Vehicle are perhaps best characterised as an uncommon form of 'The Great Vehicle' since they share the same spiritual goal.

List of Names

Dharmakirti
Sixth-century CE Indian master, who authored major works on logic and epistemology, such as *Ascertaining Valid Cognition*. Sakya Pandita (see below) did much to introduce Dharmakirti's thought in Tibet.

Jamgon Ju Mipham (1846–1912)
One of the greatest philosophers of the Nyingma school in Tibet, he was instrumental in reviving the intellectual inheritance of his tradition. Also known as Mipham Rinpoche.

Jetsun Drakpa Gyaltsen (1147–1216)
Third of the five founding masters of the Sakya school of Tibetan Buddhism and son of Sachen Kunga Nyingpo (see below). He was an extraordinarily accomplished practitioner of the tantras, composing numerous works on this system.

Karmapa Rangjung Dorje (1284–1339)
The third of the (to date) seventeen Black Hat Karmapa hierarchs who have led the Karma Kagyu school. Rangjung Dorje authored a number of works which shaped the philosophical and tantric orientation of his school down to the present day.

Langri Thangpa (1054–1123)

An influential teacher from the early Kadam school and author of *The Eight Verses of Mind Training*, an exposition of the eponymous system of spiritual practice, which became popular in all schools of Tibetan Buddhism.

Nagarjuna

This first- and second-century CE south Indian master of 'The Great Vehicle' was one of the greatest philosophers in Buddhist history and was instrumental in establishing the Middle Way ('Madhyamaka') system of tenets.

Patrul Rinpoche (1808–1887)

A beloved master from the Nyingma school, who, rejecting monastic office, spent most of his life as a wandering yogin. He authored numerous works on 'The Great Perfection', the central contemplative system of his school.

Sachen Kunga Nyingpo (1092–1158)

The first of the founding masters of the Sakya school, who, having received a remarkably rich education from his masters, transmitted key teachings such as 'The Path and its Fruit' and 'Parting from the Four Attachments' to his own sons Sonam Tsemo and Jetsun Drakpa Gyaltsen (see above).

Sakya Pandita (1182–1251)

The fourth of the founding masters of the Sakya school, his scholarship, in both religious and secular fields of learning, marks him as one of the truly defining figures of Buddhism and Tibetan culture.

Saraha

One of the most influential mediaeval Indian tantric masters, whose teachings have been preserved in a number of poetic song cycles known as 'doha'. He is an important spiritual predecessor of the Kagyu schools in Tibet, whose famed yogin and poet Milarepa (1040–1123) is sometimes dubbed 'The Tibetan Saraha'.

Shamar Konchog Yenlag (1526–1583)
The fifth of the Red Hat Karmapa hierarchs from the Karma Kagyu school. He was the author of a number of celebrated works on various sutra and tantra topics.

Shantideva
An eighth-century Indian master whose *Entering the Bodhisattva Path* became one of the most influential works on the ethics of 'The Great Vehicle'.

Thokme Zangpo (1295–1369)
A master from the Sakya and Kadam traditions, who authored popular expositions of the system of 'Mind Training' and the bodhisattva path.

Vasubandhu
A fourth-century Kashmiri master, who, together with his half-brother Asanga, elaborated the theories of the 'Mind Only' ('Chittamatra') philosophical school.

Notes

Introduction

1   The Shakyas were a clan who flourished during the latter part of the Vedic period of Indian civilisation (approximately 1750–400 BCE). Their capital was Kapilavastu, located, probably, in present-day Nepal, although some claim that it was, in fact, located in the territory of the modern state of India. Unusually for the period, the Shakya polity was a type of oligarchical republic. In fact, Shuddhodhana, the father of the Buddha, served as an elected raja; thus it is not entirely incorrect to style Buddha a 'prince'.

Chapter Two

2   For a general account of the Reformation, see Owen Chadwick, *The Reformation* (Penguin: London, 1972). For a selection from Luther's own works, see E.G. Rupp and B. Drewery (eds.), *Martin Luther* (Edward Arnold: London, 1970).

3   On the influence of Protestantism upon the expansion of Capitalism see Max Weber, *The Protestant Ethic and the Spirit of Capitalism* (Oxford University Press: Oxford, 2010).

4   The standard account of the Anabaptist revolutionaries of this period is found in Norman Cohn, *The Pursuit of*

the Millennium: Revolutionary Millenarians and Mystical Anarchists of the Middle Ages (Paladin: London, 1970).

5 On the role of the new intellectuals see Gerald R. Cragg, *The Church and the Age of Reason 1648–1789* (Penguin, London: 1977) and Robert Mandrou, *From Humanism to Science: 1480–1700* (Penguin, London: 1978).

6 For a brief but lucid introduction to Descartes, see Roger Scruton, *A Short History of Modern Philosophy: From Descartes to Wittgenstein* (Routledge, London: 1972).

7 Thomas Aquinas (1225–1279) was an Italian member of the Dominican order and the most influential philosopher in Catholic history. His system of thought, known subsequently as 'Thomism', was a synthesis of Christian thought with the work of the Greek philosopher Aristotle, and represented a shift away from the Platonism of earlier Christian thinkers such as Augustine.

8 Mary Shelley, *Frankenstein: Or the Modern Prometheus* (Wordsworth Classics: Ware, 1992).

9 The American philosopher Thomas Nagel has described the nature of scientism in his *Mind and Cosmos: Why the Materialist Neo-Darwinian Conception of Nature is Almost Certainly False* (Oxford University Press: Oxford, 2012).

10 On the Lokayata school, see S.N. Dasgupta, *A History of Indian Philosophy* (Cambridge University Press: Cambridge, 1955).

11 On Hesychasm see J. Meyendorff, *St. Gregory Palamas and Orthodox Spirituality* (St. Vladimir's Seminary Press: Crestwood, NY, 1980).

12 On Meister Eckhart, the most celebrated of the mediaeval Rhineland Catholic mystics, see Meister Eckhart, *Selected Writing*, ed. and trans. Oliver Davies (Penguin: London, 1994).

13 On Kabbalah, see Gershom Scholem, *Major Trends in Jewish Mysticism* (Schocken Books: New York, 1941).

Chapter Four

14 See B. Victoria, *Zen at War*, 2nd Ed. (Rowman & Littlefield: Lanham, MD, 2006).

15 On the history of religion in Tibet and politics, see Sam van Schaik, *Tibet: A History* (Yale University Press: New Haven, 2011), and Tsepon W.D. Shakabpa, *Tibet: A Political History* (Yale University Press: New Haven, 1967).

16 Jean-Jacques Rousseau, *The Social Contract* (Penguin: London, 1968), 49.

17 V.I. Lenin, *Collected Works*, 4th English Ed., vol. 31, (Progress Publishers: Moscow, 1965), 408–426.

18 Francis Fukuyama, *The End of History and the Last Man* (Free Press: New York, 1992).

19 'Blind Willie McTell' in Bob Dylan, *The Lyrics* (Simon & Schuster: New York, 2014), 670.

20 'Desolation Row' in id., 221.

21 Ezra Pound, 'Hugh Selwyn Mauberley' in *The Selected Poems* (Faber & Faber: London, 1977), 100.

22 'The Ballad of Frankie Lee and Judas Priest' in Bob Dylan,

op. cit., 282.

23 T.W.D. Shakabpa, op. cit., 63.

24 Id., 95.

Chapter Five

25 Patrul Rinpoche lists the six stains as: pride, lack of faith, laziness, distraction, inward withdrawal and discouragement. See rDza dPal sprul, *sNying thig sngon 'gro'i khrid yig kun bzang bla ma'i zhal lung* (People's Publishing House: Lhasa, 1988), 14–18.

26 For a prohibition of abortion in the scriptures concerning ethical discipline see *dGe slong so sor thar pa'i mdo*, in bKa' 'gyur, vol. ca. Ladakhi Palace Edition, 9-10. For the prohibition in the tantric literature, see Grags pa rGyal mtshan, *rTsa ba'i ltung ba bcu bzhi pa'i 'grel ba gsal byed 'khrul spong* in Sa skya'i bka' 'bum, vol. 7 (Ngawang Topgay: New Delhi, 1992), 278.

27 As quoted in sGam po pa, *Dam chos yid bzhin nor bu thar pa rin po che'i rgyan* (Karma Chogar, Rumtek, 1972), 27A.

28 Sa skya Pandita, *sDom gsum rab tu bye ba'i bstan bcos* in Sa skya'i bka' 'bum, vol. 12 (Ngawang Topgay: New Delhi, 1992), 79.

29 rDza dPal sprul, op. cit., 19.

Chapter Six

30 Devadatta was the cousin of the Buddha who, due to his jealousy, engineered much strife in the nascent Buddhist community, before his eventual repentance.

31 Sa skya Pandita, op. cit., 84.

32 There is an incomplete collection of texts on this cycle of teachings located in 'jam mgon Kong sprul ed., *gDams ngag mdzod*, vol. 6 (Lama Ngodrup and Sherab Drimay: Paro, 1979–1981).

33 As quoted in Sa skya Pandita, *sDom gsum rab tu bye ba'i bstan bcos* in Sa skya'i bka' 'bum, vol. 12 (Ngawang Topgay: New Delhi, 1992), 17.

34 rJe btsun Grags pa rGyal mtshan, *gDams ngag mdzod*, vol. 6, 311.

35 Id., 312.

Chapter Seven

36 As quoted in ibid.

37 Sa skya Pandita, *Legs bshad rin po che'i* in Sa skya'i bka' 'bum, vol. 10 (Ngawang Topgay: New Delhi, 1992), 215.

38 'jam mgon Mi pham, *Nges shes rin po che'i sgron ma* (Tashijong: Palampur, n.d.), 12A.

39 For a brief explanation on the role of the lama, see Lama Jampa Thaye, *Diamond Sky: A Brief Introduction to the Buddhist Path* (Ganesha Press: Bristol, 2016), 9.

Chapter Eight

40 Nagarjuna, *Shes pa'i spring yig* in Karma Thinley Rinpoche, *The Telescope of Wisdom* (Ganesha Press: Bristol, 2009), 69.

41 Id.,14.

42 Karma pa Rang byung rDo rje, *Phyag chen smon lam*, in Situpa and Karmapa, *Mahamudra Teachings of The Supreme Siddhas* (Snow Lion: Ithaca, NY, 1995), 31.

43 'jam mgon Mi pham, op. cit., 12A.

44 Shantideva, *Byang chub sems dpa'i spyod pa la 'jug pa* (Karma Chogar: Rumtek, n.d.), 45A.

Chapter Nine

45 As quoted in Ngor chen dKon mchog Lhun grub, *sNang gsum mdzes par byed pa'i rgyan* in The Great Collection of The Lam Dre Tsogshe Teachings, vol. 30 (Sachen International: Delhi, 2008), 340.

46 Saraha, *Do ha mdzod* in 'jam mgon Kong sprul, op. cit., vol. 7, 9.

47 Shantarakshita, *dBu ma'i rgyan*, in Ju Mipham, *Speech of Delight* (Snow Lion: Ithaca, NY, 2004).

48 Nagarjuna, op. cit., 77.

49 Lang ri Thang pa Ye shes rDo rje, *Blo sbyong tshig rgyad ma* in 'jam mgon Kong sprul, op. cit., vol. 4, 165.

50 Nagarjuna, op. cit., 79.

51 Thogs med bZang po, *rGyal sras lag len so bdun ma* (Shes bya gSar khang: Dharamsala, n.d.), 6.

52 William Shakespeare, Sonnet 116: 'Let me not to the marriage of true minds'.

53 As quoted in Ngor chen dKon mchog Lhun grub, op. cit., 302.

54 Sa skya Pandita, *rDo rje theg pa's rtsa ba ltung ba*, in Sa skya'i bka' 'bum, vol. 12, 332.

55 As quoted in dKon mchog Lhun grub, op. cit., 340.

56 William Blake, *The Works of William Blake* (Wordsworth Editions: Ware, 1995), 303.

57 A brief reference to Mune Tsenpo is found in Dhongthog Rinpoche, *The Sakya School of Tibetan Buddhism* (Wisdom: Boston, 2016), 42.

58 Shamar Konchok Yenlak, *A Concise Lojong Manual* (Bird of Paradise Press: Lexington, VA, 2014), 22.

59 rDza dPa sprul, op. cit., 477.

60 Shantideva, op. cit., 36A.

61 Id., 13A.

62 See Lama Jampa Thaye, *Rain of Clarity* (Ganesha Press: Bristol, 2012), 41.

63 See id., 83, and Lama Jampa Thaye, *Diamond Sky*, op. cit., 47.

Chapter Ten

64 Padmasambhava, also known as 'The Precious Guru', was the eighth-century yogin from Oddiyana (the present-day Swat valley of northern Pakistan), who, due to his mastery of the tantras, was able to play a major role in the transmission of Buddhism to Tibet alongside the philosopher Shantarakshita.

75065420R00079

Made in the USA
Columbia, SC
10 August 2017